MEDIAEVAL SOURCES IN TRANSLATION 6

POETRIA NOVA

OF

GEOFFREY OF VINSAUF

translated by

MARGARET F. NIMS

PONTIFICAL INSTITUTE OF MEDIAEVAL STUDIES

Toronto — Canada

1967

LIBRARY AND ARCHIVES CANADA CATALOGUING IN PUBLICATION

Geoffrey, of Vinsauf, fl. 1200
    Poetria nova / of Geoffrey of Vinsauf ; translated by
Margaret F. Nims.

(Mediaeval sources in translation, ISSN 0316–0874 ; 6)
Translation from the Latin.
Includes bibliographical references.
ISBN 978–0–88844–255–0

    1. Poetics – Early works to 1800.   I. Nims, Margaret F.
II. Pontifical Institute of Mediaeval Studies.   III. Title.   IV. Series.

PA8442.V5P613 2007   808.1   C2007–903789–5

First published 1967
Reprinted 2007

Pontifical Institute of Mediaeval Studies
59 Queen's Park Crescent East
Toronto, Ontario, Canada M5S 2C4

www.pims.ca

MANUFACTURED IN CANADA

TABLE OF CONTENTS

FOREWORD

The task of translating the *Poetria Nova* is an extraordinarily difficult one not only because the latinity is deliberately erudite and consciously involved, but because the erudition and the involvement so pertain to the structure of Latin that they are not transferable to a vulgar tongue.

One may be disposed to ask whether the job of translating Geoffrey of Vinsauf is really worth doing at all. It is not worth doing if not done superbly well. Done well, however, a translation of the *Poetria Nova* can remove many current misconceptions about the nature of medieval rhetoric and poetics, and this the present translation does. How many there are who feel that the applying of rhetoric to poetics is at best a game! How many quickly rise to the bait of Chaucer's teasing apostrophe to Geoffrey in the Nun's Priest's Tale! And, as a result, how many are convinced that we are in contact here with an extravagance that language today may well forego! Yet, this is not quite correct. Geoffrey had two canons which Chaucer, for all his teasing, was careful to observe. First, there is such a thing as elegant style. One is constantly aware of the truth of this whether reading the *Manchester Guardian* against the *Daily Express* or Pogo against the Katzenjammers. Elegant style is distinguishable at ever so many levels. How well Geoffrey knew this! "You can," he says near the end of his remarks on difficult ornament, "be at once elegant and easy of discourse." The secret of style is not captured in recondite words; it is found in the ordinary speech of man saying what only superior men think: "Be not a man of lofty eloquence.... The precept of the ancients is clear: speak as the many, think as the few." The classical illustration of this principle appears in the artful sequence of figures which, in the section on easy ornament, succinctly summarizes the whole of Christian doctrine. The second canon is this: "Regard not your own capacities, but rather his with whom you are speaking." Canons like these, intelligently and artfully applied, produce beauty of expression and clarity of communication. The man who would be a pleasing and effective writer will not go far astray on Geoffrey's advice: "Theory makes the craftsman sure, experience makes him ready, and imitation of good writers makes him versatile."

The Pontifical Institute of Mediaeval Studies is pleased to put into circulation this translation made by Mother St. Francis, religious of the Institute of the Blessed Virgin Mary, Toronto. The happy blending of Mother St. Francis' training in philosophy and in English letters, to say nothing of her practical knowledge of Latin, gives this translation something of the authentic quality one expects to meet only in a new creation.

LAURENCE K. SHOOK, C.S.B.

President

The Pontifical Institute of Mediaeval Studies Toronto

INTRODUCTION

Poets, said Geoffrey of Vinsauf, are formed through a happy collaboration of three elements: *ars* — a thorough knowledge of the rules; *imitatio* — the study and imitation of great writers; and *usus* — diligent practice. The author, in writing his new *ars poetica*, hoped to provide comprehensive coverage of all three areas: he would offer precepts for the poet-in-training ; scope for practice, in the form of model exercises; and adequate criteria for a systematic analysis and appreciation of the *auctores*.

Assuming that poetics was a part of rhetoric, Geoffrey of Vinsauf organized his treatise on the model of the rhetorical manuals, considering invention briefly and then devoting more extensive treatment to arrangement, expression or style, memory, and delivery. But since grammar as well as rhetoric claimed poetics as its province, Geoffrey digressed, between his discussions of style and memory, to consider routines of verbal invention that are well within the grammarian's special discipline.

The resulting system of poetics may seem to twentieth-century judgement singularly mechanical; however, our initial attitude of condescension should perhaps be reconsidered. *Natura,* the genuine poet's native endowment, was recognized, if not analyzed, in Geoffrey's time; but *natura* without *ars* was inconceivable in the creative artist. Words were the poet's medium, and almost nothing in the sound, shape, or chiaroscuro of words taken singly or in patterned sequence, taken figuratively or literally, escaped the attention of the theorist. This is not the place for a defence of the twelfth and thirteenth-century *artes poeticae*; it is a fact, however, that they represent, and in some instances constitute, the training in expression of most of the poets of western

Europe from the thirteenth century through the Renaissance.

The emphasis on verbal expression in the *artes* does not necessarily imply, on the part of their authors, subordination of content to style. Early in his treatise Geoffrey states that *Poetria*, as an art of words, is the handmaiden of *Materia*. The relationship is affirmed still more clearly in his *Documentum de Modo et Arte Dictandi et Versificandi* (II, 3, 2): "Substance [*sententia*] must be the writer's first concern, before he turns his attention to the harmonious arrangement of words; for words are dead unless sustained by the sound vitality of substance, which is the life and soul of verbal expression". *Inventio*, however (in its broad sense, the finding of the material), was an area of discourse common to poetry and prose, and therefore special treatment in a handbook on poetics was not seen to be necessary.

The major source for Geoffrey of Vinsauf's treatise is the *Rhetorica ad Herennium*, or *Rhetorica Nova*, accepted throughout the Middle Ages as a work of Cicero's. As Geoffrey echoes the title of that work in his own, so too he indicates his second important source, Horace's *Ars Poetica*, known to the twelfth century as the *Poetria*. Writing in verse, as Horace had, Geoffrey contributes his "little work, brief in form, vast in import" to the long tradition of versified manuals in the liberal arts which extended back beyond Horace and continued long after the twelfth century.

Of Geoffrey himself, very little is known. Manuscript attributions of his treatise to "Galfridus Anglicus" seem to confirm his implied statement (*P.N.* 1.31) that he was an Englishman. His apparently authentic complaint preserved in the Hunterian Museum manuscript[1] adds two probable

---

[1] *Causa magistri Gaufredi Vinesauf,* in the Hunterian Museum manuscript 511. A transcription of this fifty-line poem was printed by Edmond Faral in *Studi Medievali* (new series) IX (1936), 56-7. See also H. G. Richardson, "The Schools of Northampton in the Twelfth Century," *English Historical Review* LVI (1941), 595-605.

biographical facts: that he had studied in Paris and taught at Hampton in England. According to the dedication of the *Poetria Nova,* he had visited Rome. Anything beyond this is conjecture.

Until further work is done on the very numerous manuscripts of the *Poetria Nova,* it will not be possible to establish precisely its date of composition. The following points are relevant:

(1) ll. 326-66 suggest a date before King Richard's death in 1199 — not conclusively, however, for the lines may be a *post factum* exercise in prophecy.

(2) ll. 368-430 were, more certainly, written shortly after Richard's death.

(3) ll. 469-507, giving the complaint of the cross, seem to be part of the preparatory campaign (well under way by 1200) for the Fourth Crusade; or possibly for the Fifth Crusade, which took place after Innocent's death in 1216. This second period seems less likely since no mention is made of the tragic Children's Crusade of 1212.

(4) ll. 517-26 have their greatest relevance between 1199 and 1204. See, however, the note on this passage.

(5) ll. 2081-98 refer most probably to the years 1212-15, although an earlier date is possible. Since these lines have no intrinsic connection with the *Poetria Nova,* and since it seems unlikely from the nature and length of the poem that it was originally composed as an occasional piece, the date suggested by the passage is valid only as a *terminus ante quem.* Indeed, the entire passage is missing from the best early manuscripts I have seen (e.g. CCC 406, Laud Misc. 515, and the three Trinity College manuscripts).

(6) ll. 2099-2116, the secondary dedication to William of Wrotham, or William of London (or some other?) may also

be a later addition, and would be appropriate for either of these men any time between 1200 and 1215.

Until further evidence appears, there seems no strong reason for assigning a date later than 1200-02 for the substantial completion of the *Poetria Nova*. Revisions, deletions, additions were probably made as late as 1215.

A great deal of work remains to be done on the Latin text of the *Poetria Nova,* and on its manuscript tradition. It is gratifying to know that a definitive edition is now being prepared. This present translation is based upon the only readily available Latin text, that of Edmond Faral in *Les arts poétiques du XII° et du XIII° siècle,* Paris, 1924. I have consulted P. Leyser's two editions of 1721 and 1724, and have examined some twenty manuscripts in English libraries. From several of the earliest and best of these I have adopted a number of readings that differ from Faral's; all such variants I have listed in an appendix. Translation has been rendered difficult at times because of the uncertainty of the text, at other times because of Geoffrey's fondness for novel metaphor. It was pleasant to discover from the glosses that even early readers of the *Poetria Nova* were occasionally baffled by the extravagance of its "transferred" meanings.

I am grateful to Professor Theodore Silverstein of the University of Chicago for encouraging this translation in its early stages; to Dr. Richard W. Hunt of the Bodleian Library for valuable advice on the manuscripts; to Professor C. R. Cheney of Corpus Christi College for placing at my disposal his great knowledge of Geoffrey's age during my visit to Cambridge; to Professor R. J. Schoeck of St. Michael's College for several helpful suggestions; and to Reverend L. K. Shook of the Pontifical Institute of Mediaeval Studies for his constant and encouraging interest in the project.

POETRIA NOVA

DEDICATION

Holy Father, wonder of the world, if I say Pope
Nocent I shall give you a name without a head;
but if I add the head, your name will be at odds
with the metre. That name seeks to resemble you:
it will no more be confined by metre than your
great virtue by the shackles of measure. There is   5
no standard by which I may measure your virtue ;
it transcends the measures of men. But divide the
name — divide the name thus: set down first
"In," then add "nocent" and it will be in friendly
accord with the metre. In the same way your
excellence, if it is divided up, is equalled by many,
but taken in its wholeness it is equalled by none.
In illustrious lineage you compare with Bartho-   10
lomew; in gentle heart, with Andrew; in precious
youth, with John; in firm faith, with Peter; in
perfect knowledge, with Paul. In these qualities
taken together, there is no one with whom to
compare you. One of your gifts remains to be
mentioned which heaven allows no one to approach: the grace of your eloquence. Silence,
Augustine ! Pope Leo, be still ! Cease, John !   15
Gregory, stay your speech ! Why should I specify
all these ? Granted that one man or another may
be golden-tongued and brilliant in discourse, yet
his speech is inferior to yours, and the gold of your
eloquence sets its own precedent. You quite

20 transcend the human condition: where will physical youthfulness like yours be found in a man of such age, or where a heart so mature implanted in one so young ? What strange conflict in the nature of things: a youth of ripe age ! Although, when the era of faith began, the Lord set John above Peter
25 in love, yet he chose to set Peter above John in the papacy. In you, Holy Father, an unheard of thing has now, in our days, come to pass: a pope who is Peter the elder, and a pope who is John the youth. Your retinue — fit men for a man so great — radiate and glow round the pope as
30 stars round the sun. You alone are like the world's sun, they like its stars, Rome like the heavens. England sent me to Rome as from earth to heaven; it sent me to you as from darkness to light. General light of this world, deign to shed your lustre upon me. Most gracious of men, share your gracious-
35 ness with one who is yours. Only you can and must, only you desire and know how to give with munificence: know how to, in that you are prudent; wish to, in that you are gracious; must, in that you are high-born; can, in that you are pope. Since you are so good and so great, here has my mind come to rest after journeying far and wide;
40 in giving what it has to offer it prefers you alone to all others; it dedicates to you all it is capable of. Receive, great man, this little work, brief in form, vast in power.

I. General Remarks on Poetry
Divisions of the Present Treatise

Invention of the
poem's substance

If a man has a house to build, his impetuous hand does not rush into action. The measuring line

of his mind first lays out the work, and he mentally 45
outlines the successive steps in a definite order.
The mind's hand shapes the entire house before
the body's hand builds it. Its mode of being is
archetypal before it is actual. Poetic art may see
in this analogy the law to be given to poets: let the
poet's hand not be swift to take up the pen, nor his 50
tongue be impatient to speak; trust neither hand
nor tongue to the guidance of fortune. To ensure
greater success for the work, let the discriminating
mind, as a prelude to action, defer the operation of
hand and tongue, and ponder long on the subject
matter. Let the mind's interior compass first circle 55
the whole extent of the material. Let a definite
order chart in advance at what point the pen will
take up its course, or where it will fix its Cadiz.
As a prudent workman, construct the whole fabric
within the mind's citadel; let it exist in the mind
before it is on the lips.

When due order has arranged the material in the 60   Invention of
hidden chamber of the mind, let poetic art come   verbal expression
forward to clothe the matter with words. Since
poetry comes to serve, however, let it make due
preparation for attendance upon its mistress. Let
it take heed lest a head with tousled locks, or a
body in rumpled garments, or any final details
prove displeasing, and lest in adorning one part it 65
should in some way disfigure another. If any
part is ill-groomed, the work as a whole incurs
censure from that one part. A touch of gall makes
all the honey bitter; a single blemish disfigures the
entire face. Give careful thought to the material, 70
therefore, that there may be no possible grounds
for reproach.

Let the poem's beginning, like a courteous attendant, introduce the subject with grace. Let the main section, like a diligent host, make provision for its worthy reception. Let the conclusion, like a herald when the race is over, dismiss it honour-
75 ably. In all of its parts let the whole method of presentation bring credit upon the poem, lest it falter in any section, lest its brightness suffer eclipse.

Divisions of the present treatise

In order that the pen may know what a skilful ordering of material requires, the treatise to follow begins its course with a discussion of order. Since the following treatise begins its course with a
80 discussion of order, its first concern is the path that the ordering of material should follow. Its second care: with what scales to establish a delicate balance if meaning is to be given the weight appropriate to it. The third task is to see that the body of words is not boorishly crude but urbane. The final concern is to ensure that a well-modulated
85 voice enters the ears and feeds the hearing, a voice seasoned with the two spices of facial expression and gesture.

II. Ordering the Material

Natural order and the order of art

The material's order may follow two possible courses: at one time it advances along the pathway of art, at another it travels the smooth road of nature. Nature's smooth road points the way when "things" and "words" follow the same sequence,
90 and the order of discourse does not depart from the order of occurrence. The poem travels the pathway of art if a more effective order presents first what was later in time, and defers the appearance of

what was actually earlier. Now, when the natural order is thus transposed, later events incur no censure by their early appearance, nor do early events by their late introduction. Without con- 95 tention, indeed, they willingly assume each other's place, and gracefully yield to each other with ready consent. Deft artistry inverts things in such a way that it does not pervert them; in transposing, it disposes the material to better effect. The order of art is more elegant than natural order, and in excellence far ahead, even though it puts last 100 things first.

The first branch of order has no offshoots; the second is prolific: from its marvelous stock, bough branches out into boughs, the single shoot into many, the one into eight. The air in this region of art may seem murky and the pathway rugged, the 105 doors locked and the theory itself entangled with knots. Since that is so, the words that follow will serve as physicians for that disorder. Scan them well: here you will find a light to dispel the darkness, safe footing to traverse rugged ground, a key to unlock the doors, a finger to loose the knots. The 110 way is thrown open; guide the reins of your mind as the nature of your course demands.

Natural order has one form only; the order of art has eight forms

Let that part of the material which is first in the order of nature wait outside the gates of the work. Let the end, as a worthy precursor, be first to enter and take up its place in advance, as a guest of more honourable rank, or even as master. 115 Nature has placed the end last in order, but art respectfully defers to it, leads it from its humble position and accords it the place of honour.

The order of art begins :

1 with the end

The place of honour at the beginning of a work

2 with the middle

does not reserve its lustre for the end of the material only; rather, two parts share the glory: the end of
120 the material and the middle. Art draws from either of these a graceful beginning. Art plays, as it were, the conjurer: causes the last to be first, the future to be present, the oblique to be straight, the remote to be near; what is rustic becomes urbane, what is old becomes new, public things are made
125 private, black things white, and worthless things are made precious.

3-5 with a proverb, drawn from beginning, middle, or end

If a still more brilliant beginning is desired (while leaving the sequence of the material unchanged) make use of a proverb, ensuring that it may not sink to a purely specific relevance, but raise its head high to some general truth. See that, while prizing the charm of the unusual, it may not con-
130 centrate its attention on the particular subject, but refuse, as if in disdain, to remain within its bosom. Let it take a stand above the given subject, but look with direct glance towards it. Let it say nothing directly about the subject, but derive its inspiration therefrom.

This kind of beginning is threefold, springing up
135 from three shoots. The shoots are the first, the middle, and the last parts of the theme. From their stem a sprig, as it were, bursts forth, and is thus wont to be born, one might say, of three mothers. It remains in hiding, however, and when summoned it refuses to hear. It does not as a rule come forward
140 when the mind bids it; it is of a somewhat haughty nature, and does not present itself readily nor to all. It is reluctant to appear, unless, indeed, it is compelled to do so.

Proverbs, in this way, add distinction to a poem. 6-8 with an exemplum drawn from beginning, middle, or end No less appropriately do exempla occupy a position at the beginning of a work. The same quality, indeed, shines forth from exempla and proverbs, and the distinction conferred by the two is of equal value. In stylistic elegance, proverbs alone are 145 on a par with exempla. Artistic theory has advanced other techniques [for the poem's beginning] but prefers these two; they have greater prestige. The others are of less worth and more recent appearance; the sanction of time favours the two forms mentioned. Thus the way that lies open is more restricted, its use more appropriate, its art superior, 150 as we see both from artistic principle and from practice.

Three branches of [artistic] beginning have thus been discovered by careful search: end, middle, and proverbs. A fourth branch is the exemplum; but this one, too, like the one before it, rises up in three shoots. In these eight branches the pen itself takes pride.

That your eyes may see as witness what we have 155   Exemplary said to your ears, consider the brief story that has   exercises as its first part Minos, its second the death of his son, its conclusion the thwarting of Scylla.

Natural order begins the story in some way like   Natural beginning this:

Aside from the bounty of Fortune, whose lavish gifts flow forth as from a torrent, Nature, with other splendour, 160 *prospers the glory of Minos. She arms his body with exceptional strength and adorns his limbs with rare beauty. She refines alike the gold of his mind and the silver of his tongue. She polishes each detail to perfection, infusing a marvelous charm of manner. Such grace as befits a king* 165 *is reflected alike in every part of his nature.*

Artistic beginning :
1 with the end

Art draws a beginning for the poem from the end of the story, thus:

By the treason of Scylla was Scylla betrayed; she was wounded by the very weapon with which she inflicted a
170 *wound. She who was false to her father failed in her longing; because she condemned, she incurred like condemnation. Fit vengeance recoiled on the source of deceit in deceit of like measure.*

2 with the middle

From the middle of the story we may fashion a beginning like this:

Spying into the mind and years of Androgeos, Envy
175 *sees in his years a boy, in his mind an old man; for, endowed with the mind of age, the boy has nothing boyish about him. From his very triumphs arise his misfortune. Since his praise soars aloft he is dashed from that height. Since his lustre is great, he labours to his own destruction, and exerts his man's mind to the doom of his youthful years.*

3 with a pro- 180
verb drawn from
the beginning

The following general statement is appropriate for the first part of the story:

What is more desirable is more evanescent. All things augur decline, and prosperity is prompter to ruin. Ever blandly, fierce chance lays its snares, and happier fortune swiftly anticipates flight.

4 with a pro- 185
verb drawn
from the middle

For the middle, this generalization is relevant:

Envy, vilest of things, wholly a mortal poison, good only for evil, malign only towards good, silently plots all malign counsel, and spreads abroad to the world whatever bitter thing it conceives.

5 with a pro- 190
verb drawn
from the end

The end of the story suggests a proverb of this sort:

Just is the law that strikes guile with grief; that turns grief back on the head whence it issued.

This illustrative image may serve for the beginning of the story:

Suddenly the grim gale rages under a joyous sky; the murky air pours rain after a sun serene.

You may choose an exemplum like this to illustrate the middle of the story:

Upon the sown seed, foster child of nursing earth, the gloomy darnel vents its rancour; it blocks the seed's will to be born, and closing its gates maliciously grudges the seed's rising.

So too, in a similar way, you may prelude the end of the story:

Often the arrow learns to rebound on the archer; and the stroke, turned aside, to recoil on the striker.

III. AMPLIFICATION AND ABBREVIATION

For the opening of the poem, the principles of art outlined above have offered a variety of paths. The poem's development now invites you onward. Keeping to our image, direct your steps further along the road's course.

The way continues along two routes: there will be either a wide path or a narrow, either a river or a brook. You may advance at a leisurely pace or leap swiftly ahead. You may report the matter with brevity or draw it out in a lengthy discourse. The footing on either path is not without effort; if you wish to be wisely guided, entrust yourself to a reliable guide. Reflect upon the precepts below; they will guide your pen and teach the essentials for each path. The material to be moulded, like the moulding of wax, is at first hard to the touch. If intense concentration enkindle native ability,

6 with an exemplum drawn from the beginning

195

7 with an exemplum drawn from the middle

200 8 with an exemplum drawn from the end

205

210

215

the material is soon made pliant by the mind's fire, and submits to the hand in whatever way it requires, malleable to any form. The hand of the mind controls it, either to amplify or curtail.

A. Amplification

Techniques of amplification

1 repetition (*interpretatio, expolitio*)

220   If you choose an amplified form, proceed first of all by this step: although the meaning is one, let it not come content with one set of apparel. Let it vary its robes and assume different raiment. Let it take up again in other words what has already been said; let it reiterate, in a number of clauses, a single thought. Let one and the same thing be concealed

225 under multiple forms — be varied and yet the same.

2 periphrasis (*circuitio, circumlocutio*)

    Since a word, a short sound, passes swiftly through the ears, a step onward is taken when an expression made up of a long and leisurely sequence of sounds is substituted for a word. In order to amplify the poem, avoid calling things by their names; use

230 other designations for them. Do not unveil the thing fully but suggest it by hints. Do not let your words move straight onward through the subject, but, circling it, take a long and winding path around what you were going to say briefly. Retard the tempo by thus increasing the number of words.

235 This device lengthens brief forms of expression, since a short word abdicates in order that an extended sequence may be its heir. Since a concept is confined in one of three strongholds — in a noun, or a verb, or a combination of both — do not let the noun or verb or combination of both render the concept explicit, but let an amplified

240 form stand in place of verb or noun or both.

A third step is comparison, made in accord with one of two laws — either in a hidden or in an overt manner. Notice that some things are joined deftly enough, but certain signs reveal the point of juncture. A comparison which is made overtly presents a resemblance which signs explicitly point out. These signs are three: the words *more, less, equally*. A comparison that is made in a hidden way is introduced with no sign to point it out. It is introduced not under its own aspect but with dissembled mien, as if there were no comparison there at all, but the taking on, one might say, of a new form marvelously engrafted, where the new element fits as securely into the context as if it were born of the theme. The new term is, indeed, taken from elsewhere, but it seems to be taken from there; it is from outside and does not appear outside; it makes an appearance within and is not within; so it fluctuates inside and out, here and there, far and near; it stands apart, and yet is at hand. It is a kind of plant; if it is planted in the garden of the material the handling of the subject will be pleasanter. Here is the flowing water of a well-spring, where the source runs purer; here is the formula for a skilful juncture, where the elements joined flow together and touch each other as if they were not contiguous but continuous; as if the hand of nature had joined them rather than the hand of art. This type of comparison is more artistic; its use is much more distinguished.

In order that you may travel the more spacious route, let apostrophe be a fourth mode of delay. By it you may cause the subject to linger on its way, and in it you may stroll for an hour. Take

Marginal notes:

3 comparison (*collatio*)

(a) overt (*aperta*) 245

(b) hidden (*occulta*)

250

255

260

4 apostrophe (*apostrophatio, exclamatio*)

265

delight in apostrophe; without it the feast would be ample enough, but with it the courses of an excellent cuisine are multiplied. The splendour of dishes arriving in rich profusion and the leisured delay at the table are festive signs. With a variety

270 of courses we feed the ear for a longer time and more lavishly. Here is food indeed for the ear when it arrives delicious and fragrant and costly. Example may serve to complement theory: the eye is a surer arbiter than the ear. One example is not enough; there will be an ample number; from this ample

275 evidence learn what occasion suitably introduces apostrophe, what object it addresses, and in what form.

Model exercises

(1)

Rise up, apostrophe, before the man whose mind soars too high in prosperity, and rebuke him thus:

Why does joy so intense excite your spirit? Curb jubilation with due restraint and extend not its limits

280 *beyond what is meet. O soul, heedless of misfortune to come, imitate Janus: look to past and to future; if your venture has prospered, regard not beginnings but issues. From the sun's setting appraise the day, not from its rising. To be fully secure, fear the future. When you*

285 *think that you have done all, the serpent lurks in the grass. Keep in mind, as example, the sirens; learn from them in a happier time ever to beware an unhappy. There is nothing stable in things of this world: after honey comes poison; dark night brings the day to a close, and clouds end*

290 *calm weather. Though happily all man's affairs are subject to change, misfortune is wont to return with greater alacrity.*

(2)

If vaunting presumption impudently puffs up a man, pour the oil of mild words on his swelling pride:

Let your eyes go ahead of your footsteps; take stock of
your mind and measure your strength. If you are strong, 295
dare great things; if you are weak, lay lighter burdens
upon your shoulders; if your strength is but moderate,
love what is moderate. Assume nothing which you are
presumptuous in assuming. In all things virtue is one:
to heed your true measure. Firmly imprint on your mind :
although you are greater than others, feign yourself less, 300
and deceive yourself in your own regard. Do not thus
hurl others down to the depths, nor rate yourself above the
heavens. Let deeds surpass words ; boasting diminishes
fame.

If the timid man should give free rein to fear in   (3)
time of adversity, come to his aid with this potent 305
resource of words:

Fear not. If perchance you do fear, assume the spirit of
one temporarily fearful, not of one habitually timid.
Let fear be a guest when it enters the gates of the mind,
not a permanent resident. Learn how to fear: if you fear,
fear without witness, and let not your countenance know 310
the fear of your mind; for if fear in your heart feeds on
and wastes your features, a happier spirit fosters and
fattens your enemy; and the grief that is sucking your limbs
dry heaps up joy for your foe. More advisedly, therefore,
if fear casts down your spirit, let a happy deceit lift up
your head, and with the shield of brave features succour 315
your fear; so, if the mind is afraid, the countenance may
will to be feared. Nay, rather, will to be hopeful; and
let it be shame, for one who is fearing, to grow pale with
mean-spirited dread. If it is possible, dilate the soul that
is straitened. If the body is weak, let the spirit be strong;
take care to supplement limited physical strength with 320
great hope. An easy deed is made heavy for one who
rebels against it, and a heavy deed becomes light for the

willing mind. Will it, therefore, and to have no fears will be easy.

(4)

325

In time of success, time of auspicious fortune, you may say these words as presage of grief to come:

Queen of kingdoms while King Richard lives, England, whose glory spreads afar a mighty name, you to whom is left the world's dominion, your position is secure under so
330 *great a helmsman. Your king is the mirror in which, seeing yourself, you take pride; the star, with whose radiance you shine; the pillar, whose support gives you strength; the lightning which you send against foes; the glory by which you almost attain the height of the gods. But why do I mention details? Nature could not*
335 *have made one greater than he, and willed not to make his peer. But let no reliance at all be placed in human strength; death breaks what is brave. Have no faith in your omens; if they have shone briefly upon you, soon stormy fate will bring to a close the calm day, and the shadows of twilight*
340 *will usher in night. Soon now will be shattered that mirror which it is your glory to view; that star will suffer eclipse by whose light you shine; that pillar will shudder and crash whence you now draw your strength; that lightning will cease to flash which now makes your enemies tremble; and you who are queen will be slave. Happy omens are*
345 *about to bid you farewell: you are at ease now, soon you will toil; now you laugh, you will weep; you are wealthy, you will be in need; now you are flourishing, soon you will wither; you have being now, you will scarcely even have that. But how will you know it? What will you do? Will your ear interpret the singing of birds — or their movements your eye? Will you question the fates of Apollo?*
350 *Away with astrologers! Deaf is the augur, the soothsayer blind, and the prophet mad. To know present things is*

permitted to man; God alone knows the future. Let augury's ancient error return to its native place — its home is not here; and let the heathen father of falsehood feed what he begot; for sound faith removes from the 355 *light of the Church the tripods of Phoebus and the throne of the Sibyl. You can foreknow this one thing: that no power can be lasting; that fortune ordains short life for prosperity. If you wish examples, consider the fates of your elders. The flowering prosperity of earlier times* 360 *has withered away: Minos overthrew Athens; the son of Atreus, Ilium; Scipio, the forts of great Carthage; and many a man conquered Rome. Fate's game of chance was reversed in short order. Short is the space between happy omens and sad; night is the neighbor of day.* 365 *The fates of others teach this, but your own fates will teach you.*

In time of grief, express your grief with these words: (5)

Once defended by King Richard's shield, now un-defended, O England, bear witness to your woe in the gestures of sorrow. Let your eyes flood with tears, and 370 *pale grief waste your features. Let writhing anguish twist your fingers, and woe make your heart within bleed. Let your cry strike the heavens. Your whole being dies in his death; the death was not his but yours. Death's rise was not in one place only but general. O tearful day of Venus! O bitter star! That day was your night; and that* 375 *Venus your venom. That day inflicted the wound; but the worst of all days was that other — the day after the eleventh — which, cruel stepfather to life, destroyed life. Either day, with strange tyranny, was a murderer. The besieged one pierced the besieger; the sheltered one, him* 380 *without cover; the cautious one pierced the incautious; the well-equipped soldier pierced an unarmed man —*

apostrophe to England

— to the day

— to the mur-derer

*his own king! O soldier, why, treacherous soldier, soldier
of treachery, shame of the world and sole dishonour of
warfare; O soldier, his own army's creature, why did you*

385 *dare this against him? Why did you dare this crime, this*

— to death   *hideous crime? O sorrow! O greater than sorrow! O
death! O truculent death! Would you were dead, O
death! Bold agent of a deed so vile, how dare you recall
it? You were pleased to remove our sun, and condemn
day to darkness. Do you realize whom you snatched from*

390 *us? To our eyes he was light; to our ears, melody; to our
minds an amazement. Do you realize, impious death,
whom you snatched from us? He was the lord of warriors,
the glory of kings, the delight of the world. Nature
knew not how to add any further perfection; he was the
utmost she could achieve. But that was the reason you*

395 *snatched him away: you seize precious things, and vile*

— to nature   *things you leave as if in disdain. And Nature, of you I
complain; for were you not, when the world was still
young, when you lay new-born in your cradle, giving zealous
attention to him? And that zeal did not flag before your*

400 *old age. Why did such strenuous effort bring this wonder
into the world, if so short an hour stole the pride of that
effort away? You were pleased to extend your hand to
the world and then to withdraw it; to give thus, and then
to recall your gift. Why have you vexed the world?
Either give back to us him who is buried, or give us one*

405 *like him in excellence. But you have not resources for
that; whatever you had that was wondrous or precious was
expended on him. On him were exhausted your stores of
delight. You were made most wealthy by this creature
you made; you see yourself, in his fall, most impoverished.*

410 *If you were happy before, in proportion to happiness then*

— to God   *is your misery now. If heaven allow it, I chide even God.
O God, most excellent of beings, why do you fail in your*

*nature here? Why, as an enemy would, do you strike down
a friend? If you recall, your own Joppa gives evidence
for the king — alone he defended it, opposed by so many* 415
*thousands. Acre, too, gives evidence — his power restored
it to you. The enemies of the cross add their witness —
all of them Richard, in life, inspired with such terror
that he is still feared now he is dead. He was a man
under whom your interests were safe. If, O God, you are,
as befits your nature to be, faithful and free of malice,
just and true, why then did you shorten his days? You* 420
*could have shown mercy to the world; the world was
in need of him. But you choose to have him with you,
and not with the world; you would rather favour heaven
than the world. O Lord, if it is permissible to say it,
let me say — with your leave — you could have done this* 425
*more graciously, and with less haste, if he had bridled the
foe at least (and there would have been no delay to that end;
he was on the verge of success). He could have departed
more worthily then to remain with you. But by this lesson
you have made us know how brief is the laughter of earth,* 430
how long are its tears.

If you wish to rise up in full strength against the   (6)
ridiculous, assail them in this form of speech:
offer praise, but in a facetious manner; reprove,
but with wit and grace; have recourse to gestures,
but let these be consistently fitting. Give your
speech teeth; attack with biting force — but let
your manner rather than your lips devour the   435
absurd. Lo, what was hidden in darkness will be
revealed in full light. A lively theme is under
discussion: *"Boys are raised up and made masters"*.
Let their "masterly status" evoke laughter:

Now he sits, loftily graced with the title of master, who

440 *up to now was fit for the rod. For laymen, the cap on his head guarantees him authentic; as do the cut of his robes, the gold on his fingers, his seat at the head, and the crowd in his study.*

You can laugh at the absurd situation; it is indeed a ridiculous thing:

By his own and by popular verdict this is a learned man.

445 But you perceive the same thing that I do: he is a very ape among scholars. I said that in a whisper, let no one hear it aloud. He boasts of himself, indeed, and rattling on, promises marvels. Hurry up, one and all; now the mountain's in labour, but its offspring will be only a mouse. Going before 450 him, bid the master good day; but smile, too, at times, with a sidelong glance. Mock him with the ciconia's sign of derision; or pull a wry mouth, or draw in your nostrils: for such expressions of ridicule it is fitting to use not the mouth but the nose.

455 Apostrophe varies its countenance thus: with the mien of a magistrate it rebukes vicious error; or it languishes in tearful complain ʀagainst all that is harsh; or is roused to wrath over some great crime; or appears with derisive force in attacking buffoons. When evoked by causes such as these, 460 apostrophe contributes both adornment and amplification.

5 personification   Fifth aid, personification, come forward to lengthen our route yet further. Give power of speech to that which has in itself no such power — let poetic license confer a tongue. So the earth, feeling Phaeton's heat, complained to Jove; so 465 Rome, with dishevelled hair, bewailed in tearful voice the death of Caesar. If an original example

is acceptable, consider this one; here, employing   Model exercises
personification, is the complaint of the holy cross:

I, the ravished cross, make my complaint, seized by violent   (1)
and brutish hands and defiled by the touch of curs. 470
Shamefully was I seized long ago, and I am not yet
wrested back, not yet redeemed by the sword. Tell me,
O man, did I not grow tall for you? Was I not made
fruitful for you? Did I not bear sweet fruit for you, did
I not bear salvation? Tell me, tell me, O man — tell me,
you who were lost, you whom I redeemed, did I deserve to
be thus seized without an avenger? To perish thus? 475
No hostile power, but your own sin had made possible my
seizure from you. Since I saw your numerous crimes, when
seized I willed to be seized. It was less shame to be held at
naught in an alien camp than to be so held in my own.
If your vileness was concealed from the world, yet he who 480
sees all things saw you. God fully knows your whole
being, both inside and out; and he took me from you. In
accord with rigorous law, grave vengeance ought to have
fallen upon you: death without end. But I have come,
says the merciful one, to have mercy on those who are
miserable, not to insist on judgement. I have come to 485
spare, not to punish. Take heed! Come to your senses!
Turn back at last lest you perish, O Sunamite! If you
but turn, I shall turn to you, and return with fervour to
your returned heart. Rise up at once, make haste, the
hour compels and impels you. Why do you sleep? Awake! 490
If the holy cross has redeemed you, redeem the cross by the
sword; become thereby the redeemer of that by which you
were redeemed. What sane man fails to respond to what
is for his benefit? Our Lord toiled on the cross; does the
servant rest? Take up your own cross; he took up his.
He tasted the bitter chalice; you do the same! Surely 495
consideration for the servant will not surpass that for his

Lord? If you wish to be his disciple, you must follow his sufferings with yours. Heaven is not reached by delights. Render therefore to God that death you must needs pay to 500 *nature: die in him. Since escape from death is impossible, make of necessity a virtue. Let my cause be martial for you, even though it be mortal. If you are vanquished, by that very defeat you are victor; for indeed to be vanquished is more than to vanquish; the victor enjoys the mere hope of the crown, the vanquished enjoys its possession. Burst* 505 *asunder delays, then; silence the body's protest; set aside your pleasures; and let the ready hand be swift to take arms, and the winged will chafe at delays.*

(2)   A second example of the effective use of personification will be helpful: if, for instance, a table-cloth now worn out should say:

510   *I was once the pride of the table, while my youth was in its first flower and my face knew no blemish. But since I am old, and my visage is marred, I do not wish to appear. I withdraw from you, table; farewell!*

In this way, personification employs two tones: at one time its speech is serious, at another jocose.

(3)   515   If this early example is not sufficient, here is a recent one. A proud fortress, rising up on the brow of a hill, seemed to speak thus to the French:

Why, O France, do you brag? What grounds for the menace and pride of your speech? Away with your arrogance! Unlearn your threatening gestures! Why the 520 *shields at your side, or the spears, or the swords? Womanish rabble, abandon your manly maneuvers, that your bearing may accord with your deeds. Strip off the shield and the helmet's cone. It becomes your ilk to spin the weighed wool and to empty the distaff. Why, then, or* *520 *of what do you boast? Put a curb on your tongue; fear to utter your insolent words. I will bridle your jaws, and*

throw chains on your neck, and in a short time I will
make you a slave. I am engaged in a mere trifle when I
meet you, the would-be minion of Mars! Let other foes
rise, any number you please; they are not equal to me; 525
I am rather a cause of fear to them, I who am fashioned
to the model of King Richard's heart.

If it is desirable to amplify the treatise yet more   6 digression
fully, go outside the bounds of the subject and withdraw from it a little; let the pen digress, but not
so widely that it will be difficult to find the way 530
back. This technique demands a talent marked by
restraint, lest the bypath be longer than decorum
allows. A kind of digression is made when I turn
aside from the material at hand, bringing in first
what is actually remote and altering the natural
order. For sometimes, as I advance along the
way, I leave the middle of the road, and with a
kind of leap I fly off to the side, as it were; then I 535
return to the point whence I had digressed. Lest
this matter of digression be veiled in obscurity,
I offer the following example:

The bond of a single love bound together two hearts;
a strange cause divided them one from the other. But
before they were parted, lips pressed kisses on lips; 540
a mutual embrace holds and enfolds them both. From the
fount of their eyes, tears flow down their cheeks, and sobs
alternate with farewells. Love is a spur to grief, and
grief a witness to the strength of love. Winter yields to
spring. The air unclasps its robe of cloud, and heaven 545
caresses the earth. Moist and warm, air sports with earth,
and the feminine earth feels the masculine power of the air.
A flower, earth's child, bursts forth into the breeze and
smiles at its mother. Their first foliage adorns the tips
of the trees; seeds that were dead spring up into life; 550

*the promise of harvest to come lives first in the tender blade.
Now is the season in which birds delight. This hour of
time found the lovers apart, who yet through their love
were not parted.*

7 description

Description, pregnant with words, follows as a
seventh means of amplifying the work. But al-
555 though the path of description is wide, let it also
be wise, let it be both lengthy and lovely. See
that the words with due ceremony are wedded to
the subject. If description is to be the food and
ample refreshment of the mind, avoid too curt a
brevity as well as trite conventionality. Examples
560 of description, accompanied by novel figures, will
be varied, that eye and ear may roam amid a
variety of subjects.

Model exercises

If you wish to describe, in amplified form, a
woman's beauty:

(1)

*Let the compass of Nature first fashion a sphere for
her head; let the colour of gold give a glow to her hair, and
565 lilies bloom high on her brow. Let her eyebrows resemble
in dark beauty the blackberry, and a lovely and milk-white
path separate their twin arches. Let her nose be straight,
of moderate length, not too long nor too short for perfection. Let her eyes, those watch-fires of her brow, be
570 radiant with emerald light, or with the brightness of stars.
Let her countenance emulate dawn: not red, nor yet white —
but at once neither of those colours and both. Let her
mouth be bright, small in shape — as it were, a half-circle.
Let her lips be rounded and full, but moderately so;
575 let them glow, aflame, but with gentle fire. Let her
teeth be snowy, regular, all of one size, and her breath
like the fragrance of incense. Smoother than polished
marble let Nature fashion her chin — Nature, so potent
580 a sculptor. Let her neck be a precious column of milk-*

white beauty, holding high the perfection of her coun-
tenance. From her crystal throat let radiance gleam, to
enchant the eye of the viewer and enslave his heart. Let
her shoulders, conforming to beauty's law, not slope in 585
unlovely descent, nor jut out with an awkward rise;
rather, let them be gracefully straight. Let her arms be a
joy to behold, charming in their grace and their length.
Let soft and slim loveliness, a form shapely and white, a
line long and straight, flow into her slender fingers. Let
her beautiful hands take pride in those fingers. Let her 590
breast, the image of snow, show side by side its twin
virginal gems. Let her waist be close girt, and so slim
that a hand may encircle it. For the other parts I am
silent — here the mind's speech is more apt than the 595
tongue's. Let her leg be of graceful length and her
wonderfully tiny foot dance with joy at its smallness.

So let the radiant description descend from the
top of her head to her toe, and the whole be polished
to perfection.

If you wish to add to the loveliness thus pictured 600   (2)
an account of attire:

Let her hair, braided and bound at her back, bind in its
gold; let a circlet of gold gleam on her ivory brow. Let
her face be free of adornment, lovely in its natural hue.
Have a starry chain encircle her milk-white neck. Let
the border of her robe gleam with fine linen; with gold 605
let her mantle blaze. Let a zone, richly set with bright
gems, bind her waist, and bracelets enrich her arms. Have
gold encircle her slender fingers, and a jewel more splendid
than gold shed its brilliant rays. Let artistry vie with
materials in her fair attire; let no skill of hand or in- 610
vention of mind be able to add aught to that apparel.
But her beauty will be of more worth than richness of
vesture. Who, in this torch, is unaware of the fires?

*Who does not find the flame? If Jupiter in those days
of old had seen her, he would not, in Amphitryon's shape,*
615 *have deluded Alcmena; nor assumed the face of Diana to
defraud you, Callisto, of your flower; nor would he have
betrayed Io in the form of a cloud, nor Antiope in the
shape of a satyr, nor the daughter of Agenor as a bull,
nor you, Mnemosyne, as a shepherd; nor the daughter of
Asopo in the guise of fire; nor you, Deo's daughter, in*
620 *the form of a serpent; nor Leda as a swan; nor Danae in a
shower of gold. This maiden alone would he cherish, and
see all others in her.*

(3)   But since the description of beauty is an old
and even trite theme, let the following lines serve
as model for a less common subject:

When the festal couch welcomes kings and powerful
625 *princes, the image of milk is first of the table's delights:
Ceres is honoured. Aged Bacchus grows young in goblets
of gold; alone there, or mingled with fragrant nectar,
he condescends to depart from his elegance and be merry.
A royal procession of dishes parades in on platters of gold;*
630 *courses and gold marvel at themselves and each other.
The guests note above all the paragon of the table:
his countenance vies with Paris, his youth with Partheno-
peus, with Croesus his wealth, his lineage with Caesar.
If you would note other details of his person, his linen*
635 *vies with the snow, his purple with flame, his jewel with
a star. You would observe that certain details give greater
pleasure according as they cater to the taste of the guests.
The mime has diverse attractions to woo both the eye and the
ear. His manner of entertaining is not the same for all;
each man to his taste. A varied programme has greater*
640 *appeal. The ringing sistra fly, feeding the eyes of kings;
they pass from hand to hand, and sistrum flies up to
meet sistrum. They vanish and reappear, and repeatedly*

*rise and fall. They feign threats, and conduct what looks
like a sportive battle; they fly from each other and pursue
each other. While the twin castanets are playing in the* 645
*two hands of a second mime, song plays on his lips;
nor are his feet idle — they move gracefully forward and
back and around with the same light step. Voice is the
dance's partner; song strikes the skies, the castanets clash
together, sound makes joyous assault on the ear. A third
man, agile in tumbling, whirls over in somersaults;* 650
*takes a flying leap; or with graceful bound springs erect
from a supine position; or arches his supple limbs with
his neck bent back towards his ankles. Or he raises the
point of his sword and leaps sure-footed amidst treacherous
blades. You would marvel at every exploit; but still* 655
*more enjoyable than these, now the sound of wrestling
arises: now in sport and skill fingers are locked together;
now the hand, hooked back, curves the arm into an arc at
the side, and with swift maneuver deprives the shoulders
of movement. You could see musical instruments follow* 660
*the sport, each with its own way of pleasing: the feminine
flute, the masculine trumpet, the hollow drum, the clear
bright cymbals, the mellow symphonia, the sweet-sounding
pipe, the cithera sleep-inducing, and the merry fiddle.
Warmly the guests applaud the whole entertainment;
and whatever delights are appropriate for the banquets of* 665
kings while away the hours.

In this way you may celebrate the feasts of
kings and the joys of the feast. In this way we
amplify by a long description the brief matter
proposed.

There remains yet another means of fostering   8 opposition
the amplified style: any statement at all may   (*oppositio,*
assume two forms: one form makes a positive as-   *oppositum*)
sertion, the other negates its opposite. The two 670

modes harmonize in a single meaning; and thus two streams of sound flow forth, each flowing along with the other. Words flow in abundance from the two streams. Consider this example: *"That*
675 *young man is wise."* Affirm the youthfulness of his countenance and deny its age: *"His is the appearance of youth and not of old age."* Affirm the maturity of his mind and deny its youthfulness: *"His is the mind of mature age and not of youth."* The account may perhaps continue along the same line: *"His*
680 *is not the cheek of age but of youth; his is not the mind of youth but of age."* Or, choosing details closely related to the theme, you may travel a rather long path, thus:

His face is not wrinkled, nor is his skin dry; his heart is not stricken with age, nor is his breath laboured; his
685 *loins are not stiff, nor is his back bowed; physically he is a young man, mentally he is in advanced maturity.*

In this way, plentiful harvest springs from a little seed; great rivers draw their source from a tiny spring; from a slender twig a great tree rises and spreads.

B. *Abbreviation*

Techniques of   690   If you wish to be brief, first prune away those
abbreviation   devices mentioned above which contribute to an elaborate style; let the entire theme be confined within narrow limits. Compress it in accordance
1 emphasis   with the following formula. Let *emphasis* be spokes-
2 articulus   man, saying much in few words. Let *articulus*, with
695   staccato speech, cut short a lengthy account. The
3 ablative absolute   *ablative*, when it appears alone without a pilot,
4 avoidance of   effects a certain compression. Give no quarter to
repetition   *repetition*. Let skilful *implication* convey the unsaid

in the said. Introduce no *conjunction* as a link between clauses — let them proceed uncoupled. Let the craftsman's skill effect a *fusion of many concepts in one*, so that many may be seen in a single glance of the mind. By such concision you may gird up a lengthy theme; in this bark you may cross a sea. This form of expression is preferable for a factual account, in order not to enshroud facts discreetly in mist, but rather to clear away mist and usher in sunlight. Combine these devices, therefore, when occasion warrants: emphasis, articulus, ablative absolute, deft implication of one thing in the rest, omission of conjunctions between clauses, fusion of many concepts in one, avoidance of repetition. Draw on all of these, or at least on such as the subject allows. Here is a model of abbreviation; the whole technique is reflected in it:

Her husband abroad improving his fortunes, an adulterous wife bears a child. On his return after long delay, she pretends it begotten of snow. Deceit is mutual. Slyly he waits. He whisks off, sells, and — reporting to the mother a like ridiculous tale — pretends the child melted by sun.

If a concise account is to be kept within very narrow limits, be especially careful to let every general statement lie dormant. Do not be concerned about verbs; rather, write down with the pen of the mind only the nouns; the whole force of a theme resides in the nouns. Once this has been done, follow, as it were, the technique of the metalworker. Transfer the iron of the material, refined in the fire of the understanding, to the anvil of the study. Let the hammer of the intellect make it pliable; let repeated blows of that hammer fashion

5 implication

6 asyndeton

700

7 fusion of clauses

705

710

715

720

725

from the unformed mass the most suitable words.
Let the bellows of the mind afterwards fuse those
words, adding others to accompany them, fusing
nouns with verbs, and verbs with nouns, to express
730 the whole theme. The glory of a brief work consists in this: it says nothing either more or less
than is fitting. The exercise of an unusual brevity
may be yet more pointed; the following concise
lines serve as illustration:

A husband, selling him whom the adulterous mother
feigns begotten of snow, in turn feigns him melted by sun.
735 *Since his wife feigns her offspring begotten of snow, the*
husband sells him, and likewise feigns he was melted by
sun.

IV. ORNAMENTS OF STYLE

Whether it be brief or long, a discourse should
always have both internal and external adornment, but with a distinction of ornament reflecting
the distinction between the two orders. First
740 examine the mind of a word, and only then its face;
do not trust the adornment of its face alone. If
internal ornament is not in harmony with external,
a sense of propriety is lacking. Adorning the face
of a word is painting a worthless picture: it is a false
thing, its beauty fictitious; the word is a white-
washed wall and a hypocrite, pretending to be
745 something whereas it is nothing. Its fair form con-
ceals its deformity; it makes a brave outward show,
but has nothing within. It is a picture that charms
one who stands at a distance, but displeases the
viewer who stands at close range. Take care, then,
750 not to be hasty, but be Argus in relation to what

you have said, and, Argus-eyed, examine the words
in relation to the meaning proposed. If the meaning
has dignity, let that dignity be preserved; see that
no vulgar word may debase it. That all may be
guided by precept: let rich meaning be honoured
by rich diction, lest a noble lady blush in pauper's 755
rags.

In order that meaning may wear a precious
garment, if a word is old, be its physician and give
to the old a new vigour. Do not let the word
invariably reside on its native soil — such residence
dishonours it. Let it avoid its natural location, travel 760
about elsewhere, and take up a pleasant abode
on the estate of another. There let it stay as a novel
guest, and give pleasure by its very strangeness.
If you provide this remedy, you will give to the
word's face a new youth.

1. Difficult Ornament

The method suggested above affords guidance 765
in the artistic transposition of words. If an observation is to be made about man, I turn to an object
which clearly resembles man [in the quality or state
of being I wish to attribute to him]. When I see
what that object's proper vesture is, in the aspect
similar to man's, I borrow it, and fashion for
myself a new garment in place of the old. For
example, taking the words in their literal sense, 770
gold is said to be yellow; milk, white; a rose, very
red; honey, sweet-flowing; flames, glowing; snow,
white. Say therefore: *snowy* teeth, *flaming* lips,
honied taste, *rosy* countenance, *milky* brow, *golden*
hair. These word-pairs are well suited to each 775
other: teeth, snow; lips, flames; taste, honey; countenance, rose; brow, milk; hair, gold. And since

The ten tropes

1 metaphor
(*translatio*)

(a) passage
from
things to
man

(b) passage from man to things

here the linking of aspects that are similar sheds a pleasing light, if the subject of your discourse is not man, turn the reins of your mind to the human realm. With artistic tact, transpose a word which, in its literal sense, applies to man in an analogous situation. For example, if you should wish to say: "Springtime makes the earth beautiful; the first flowers grow up; the weather turns mild; storms cease; the sea is calm, its motion without violence; the vales are deep, the mountains lofty;" consider what words, in a literal sense, express the analogous situation in our human life. When you adorn something, you *paint*; when you enter on existence, you *are born*; affable in discourse, you *placate*; withdrawing from all activity, you *sleep*; motionless, you *stand on fixed foot*; sinking down, you *lie;* lifted into the air, you *rise*. The wording is a source of pleasure, then, if you say:

Metaphorical use of verbs
780

785

790

Model exercises

(1)

Springtime p a i n t s the earth with flowers: the first blossoms a r e   b o r n; the mild weather s o o t h e s; storms, dying down, s l u m b e r; the sea s t a n d s   s t i l l, as if without movement; the valleys l i e   d e e p; the mountains r i s e   a l o f t.

795

When you transpose a word whose literal meaning is proper to man, it affords greater pleasure, since it comes from what is your own. Such a metaphor serves you as mirror, for you see yourself in it and recognize your own sheep in another's field. Consider several examples of this kind. If, for instance, we wish to describe the malignity of winter, introducing this trope:

800

(2)

Winter ever t h r e a t e n s   w i t h   m o u t h   a g a p e, harsher than harsh tyrants. At its command, storm clouds s p r e a d   g l o o m through the sky; darkness b l i n d s

t h e   e y e of day; the air g i v e s   b i r t h to tempests;
snow   c l o s e s   the roadways; hoar frost p i e r c e s 805
one's marrow; hail l a s h e s the earth; ice i m p r i-
s o n s the waves.

Or, if we would speak of weather favourable for navigation:

The north wind does not c h i d e the waters, nor the   (3)
south wind i n e b r i a t e the air; but the rays of the
sun, like a broom in the murky sky, s w e e p   c l e a n 810
the heavens; and with placid mien the season f a w n s
o n the deep; the secret murmuring of a breeze s t i l l s
the water and q u i c k e n s the sails.

Or if, in similar strain, we would speak of the metal-smith's work:

Flames w a k e n in response to the bellows; the crude   (4)
metal i s b u r i e d in fire; tongs t r a n s f e r the
heated mass directly from fire to forge; the mallet, as 815
master, d e a l s b l o w a f t e r b l o w, and with
hard strokes c h a s t i s e s the metal; and so it does what
he wishes: it d r a w s f o r t h a rounded helmet, useful
counsellor for the head; or it g e n e r a t e s a sword,
legitimate fellow for the side; or a cuirass m a k e s i t s 820
a p p e a r a n c e, friend of the body; together with these
a r e b o r n a greave, for the leg to d o n as shield, and
a spur to i n c i t e the horse, which the ankle a d o p t s
as its own; and other shapes of iron which the craftsman's
skill fashions as armour. Objects so unlike in appearance, 825
arms of such varied shape, e x h a u s t the iron. The
mallet c u r b s its blow; the forges r e g a i n t h e i r
b r e a t h, their course accomplished; the work c o m e s
to r e s t at its goal, and c o m p l e t e s t h e t a s k
prescribed.

You may transpose verbs very effectively in this 830
way; verbs so transposed will be readily visible to

Easy intelli-
gibility essential
to metaphor

the mind's eye; to transpose them so, however, requires both labour and skill. This mode of expression is at once difficult and easy: finding the word is difficult; its relevance, once it is found, is easy. Thus contrary qualities mingle, but they
835 promise peace, and, enemies once, they stay on as friends. There is a certain balance required here: the word must not be trivial, crude, or awkward; it derives charm and value from its seriousness of meaning. Its seriousness, however, must not be pompous or obscure; easiness of comprehension renders it luminous and checks bombast. Each
840 quality must temper the other. Let this be your mode of expression then: combine seriousness and easiness in such a way that the one does not detract from the other; let them be in accord with each other and enjoy the same dwelling; let harmonious discord reconcile their differences.

Metaphorical use of adjectives to sharpen the force of metaphorical verbs

In order that a transposed verb may be introduced with more finished art, see that it does not
845 enter accompanied by a noun alone. Provide it with an adjective as well, and let the adjective be such that it affords all possible aid in clearing away any obscurity there may be in the verb. If there is no obscurity, then let the adjective elucidate the verb's meaning still more fully by shedding clear
850 light upon it. For example, if, employing this manner of speech, I make some such statement as: *the laws relax,* or *the laws stiffen,* the metaphor is not yet sufficiently clear. The transposed verb hides its meaning, as it were, under a cloud; and since a verb so introduced remains in darkness, let an adjective come to its aid and shed light
855 upon it. Say rather: *the modified laws relax,* or

the stringent laws stiffen. Now the adjective adds meaning to the verb, for stringency suggests rigour and rigid laws; kindly modification tempers and mitigates laws.

But what if a transposed verb is perfectly clear in itself ? Even so, let an adjective reinforce it, 860 so that its own clarity may be doubled by that of the adjective. Granted that I speak gracefully enough if I say: *Earth quaffed more of heaven's dew than was right, and a shower lavishly dispensed it;* yet the expression will be apter and more effective if you say: *The intoxicated earth quaffed more dew than* 865 *was right, and a prodigal shower lavishly dispensed it;* for adjective and verb act as partners and cling together like ivy, as if they could not endure to be torn asunder; rather they swear a pact of unity and are friends of one mind. Discrimination of this sort 870 has imparted a fine polish to the words, removing any trace of obscurity.

An even more effective figure, surpassing the rhetorical colour just mentioned, results when the noun [or adjective] is at strife with the verb, and they clash on the surface, but beneath there is friendly and harmonious accord. Here is an 875 illustration: *The munificent man gives lavishly, but in pouring out wealth he regains it; never is his hand weary except when it rests.* And this: *Before the face of God, devout silence cries out.* Consider other areas of experience and observe that the same thing is true: when lovers quarrel, with mutual recrimina- 880 tion, harmony of spirit grows while tongues are at war; love is built on this estrangement. So, too, in the examples given above, the words are basically in accord, although on the surface they are at

Opposition of meaning between noun and verb

variance. There is opposition in the words them-
885 selves, but the meaning of the words allays all
opposition.

Alliance of literal and figurative meaning in the same word

A metaphorical word glows with a different
radiance when it is employed in a figurative and
in a literal sense at the same time, as in this example:
*That ancient practical wisdom of Rome armed tongues
with laws and bodies with iron, that it might prepare
890 tongues and bodies alike for warfare.* Or take this
example, since brevity has greater zest: *Faith arms
their hearts, iron their bodies.*

Observations on metaphor :
(a) the verb

A verb is susceptible of metaphorical meaning, so
is an adjective, so is a noun. Transposition of a
verb, however, is made in various ways: either in
895 relation to its subject, or to its complement, or to

— in relation to its subject

both at once. It is metaphorical in relation to its
subject, as in this example: *In spring time clouds
a r e   a t   r e s t, the air g r o w s   g e n t l e, the breeze
i s   s t i l l ; birds, chirping to each other, a r e   m e r r y;
900 the sea s l u m b e r s, brooks p l a y, boughs d o n   t h e
r a i m e n t   o f   y o u t h, fields a r e   p a i n t e d,*

— to its complement

the earth r e j o i c e s. In relation to its complement,
as here: *The pope, potent in words, s c a t t e r s   s e e d
from his lips when he speaks; he f e e d s the eyes thereby,
and g i v e s   d r i n k to the ears, and s a t i s f i e s
i n   a b u n d a n c e the whole mind.* In relation to

— to both

both, as in lines such as these: *When the lips of the
905 pope p r o v i d e   a   f e a s t of sweet words, attentive
ears, while he speaks, d r i n k   i n words from the speaker's
lips, and what is heard restfully s o o t h e s the mind.*

(b) the adjective
— in relation to its noun

An adjective is also transposed according to a
threefold relationship: either in relation to its
noun, which it modifies in a figurative sense, as in
910 this example: *Consider the character of a discourse,*

*whether it is r a w or o v e r d o n e, whether s u c c u -
l e n t or d r y, s h a g g y or t r i m, r o u g h or
p o l i s h e d, i m p o v e r i s h e d or s u m p t u o u s.*
Or in relation to its complement, as in the following: *What will our king do, u n a r m e d in policy,
g i r t r o u n d with hostility, d i v e s t e d of friends?*
Or in relation to both at once, as when one says
a man skilled in speech is *flowering* in eloquence;
an old man is *wasted* in years; a poor man,
slender in means.

— to its com-
plement

915

— to both

We have still to consider the transposed use of
a noun. If the noun that is transposed is common,
it confers upon diction rhetorical adornment of
this sort: *The t h u n d e r i n g of the populace roused
the city; or: a t r u m p e t of thunder, the f u r y of the
blast, the q u a r r e l i n g of the winds, the c r a s h i n g
of the sea, the r a g e of the storm.* If the noun is
proper, it is transposed either with a view to
praising or censuring by the name alone (you may
praise with such names as this: *He is a P a r i s,*
or you may censure in a similar way: *He is a
T h e r s i t e s*), or with a view to suggesting some
analogy, as for instance in an expression of this
kind: *That captain rules the ship and is our T i p h y s,*
or: *That country fellow rules the chariot, our guide and
our A u t o m e d o n.* Or I may transpose a proper
noun for another reason: that the likeness suggested
may be not a true one, but by contrast a kind of
ridicule, as when I call a man deformed in body
a *Paris*, or one cruel in heart an *Aeneas*, one of
slight strength a *Pyrrhus*, one rude in speech a
Cicero, or one who is wanton *Hippolytus*. Altered
meaning of this kind gives new vitality to a word.

(c) the noun
(i) common

920

2 onomatopoeia
(*nominatio*)

(ii) proper

3 antonomasia
(*pronominatio*)

925

4 allegory
(*permutatio*)

930

935

A simple metaphor transposes one word. Sometimes several words are transposed, as in the fol-

Multiple tropes

lowing figure: *Shepherds rob the sheep;* here you transpose two nouns, *shepherds* and *sheep;* you apply
940 the name of *shepherd* to those in authority, and the name of *sheep* to those who are subject. An entire sentence may be metaphorical, and no part of it literal, as a sentence of this kind illustrates: *He plows the shore, washes brick, beats the air.* These are some of the ways in which metaphor lends adornment to words.

945 Transpose words in the ways outlined above. Be moderate, however, not bombastic or pompous. Two elements combine here, the laudable and the laborious; to transpose a word aptly is laborious, to succeed in transposing it aptly is laudable.

When meaning comes clad in such apparel, the
950 sound of words is pleasant to the happy ear, and delight in what is unusual stimulates the mind. *Transfero, permuto, pronomino, nomino,* these verbs form from themselves verbal nouns which are the names of figures. The one term *transsumptio* in-
955 cludes them all. Take pains to provide dishes like these, together with these draughts; such feasting satisfies the ear, such draughts slake its thirst.

Art has woven other garments of less price, yet they, too, have a dignified and appropriate use. There are in all ten tropes, six in this group, four
960 mentioned above. This decade of figures adorns expression in a way we term *difficult* in that a word is taken only in its figurative and not in its literal sense. All the tropes are of one general class, distinguished by the figurative status of the words and the uncommon meaning assigned them. Lest
965 understanding be uncertain and hesitant here, the following examples will ensure confidence.

Consider a statement of this kind: *The sick man seeks a physician; the grieving man, solace; the poor man, aid.* Expression attains a fuller flowering in this trope: *Illness is in need of a physician; grief is in need of solace; poverty is in need of aid.* There is a natural charm in this use of the abstract for the concrete, and so in the change of *sick man* to *sickness, grieving man* to *grief, poor man* to *poverty.*

5 metonymy *(denominatio)*

(a) abstract for concrete

970

What does fear produce? Pallor. What does anger cause? A flush. Or what, the vice of pride? A swelling up. We refashion the statement thus: *Fear grows pale, anger flushes; pride swells.* There is greater pleasure and satisfaction for the ear when I attribute to the cause what the effect claims as its own.

(b) cause for effect

975

Let the comb's action groom the hair after the head has been washed. Let scissors trim away from the hair whatever is excessive, and let a razor give freshness to the face. In this way, art teaches us to attribute to the instrument, by a happy turn of expression, what is proper to the one who uses it. So from the resources of art springs a means of avoiding worn-out paths and of travelling a more distinguished route.

(c) instrument for user

980

Again, a statement expressed in the following way adds lustre to style: *We have robbed their bodies of steel, their coffers of silver, their fingers of gold.* The point here is not that zeugma adorns the words with its own figure of speech, but that when I am about to mention something, I withhold its form completely and mention only the material. Whereas a less elegant style mentions both, art is silent about one, and conveys both by a single term. This device brings with it three advantages: it

(d) material for object

985

990

curtails the number of words required, it constitutes a poetic adornment, and it is helpful to the metre. It curtails the number of words in that a single term is more succinct than a word-group; it constitutes a poetic adornment in that an expression of this kind is artistically more skilful; and it is helpful 995 to the metre if an oblique case, whose form the metre rejects, requires such help. This is clear from the following example: *The finger rejoices in gold.* *Gold* is a shorter sound, *a ring of gold* is longer; the latter form names the object itself, the former conveys it more artfully; in the former [*aurum*] 1000 the metre admits of oblique cases, in the latter [*annulus auri*] it rejects them.

(e) container
for content

Instead of the thing contained, name that which contains it, choosing the word judiciously whether it be noun or adjective. Introduce a noun in this way: *tippling E n g l a n d; weaving F l a n d e r s; bragging N o r m a n d y.* Try out an adjective thus : *c l a-* 1005 *m o r o u s market-places; s i l e n t cloisters; l a m e n t-i n g prison; j u b i l a n t house; q u i e t night; l a-b o r i o u s day.* Seek turns of expression like the following: *In time of sickness Salerno, with its medical skill, cures those who are ill. In civil causes Bologna* 1010 *arms the defenceless with laws. Paris, in the arts, dispenses bread to feed the strong. Orleans, in its cradle, rears tender youth on the milk of the authors.*

6 hyperbole
(*superlatio*)

Give hyperbole rein, but see that its discourse does not run ineptly hither and yon. Let reason keep it in check, and its moderate use be a source 1015 of pleasure, that neither mind nor ear may shrink from excess. For example, employing this trope: *A rain of darts lashes the foe like hail; the shattered array of spears resembles a forest; a tide of blood flows like a wave of the sea, and bodies clog the valleys.* This mode of expression diminishes or heightens eulogy to a 1020 remarkable degree; and exaggeration is a source of pleasure when both ear and good usage commend it.

If you intend to say: *I studied for three years,* you may, with happier effect, adorn the statement. The wording above is inelegant and trite; you may refine the inelegant, your file may renew the trite in this way: *The third summer came upon me in 1025 study; the third autumn found me engaged; the third winter embroiled me in cares; in study I passed through three spring times.* I word the statement more skilfully when, suppressing the whole, I imply that whole from the parts, in the way just exemplified. Part of the year may be wet: *The year is wet;* part may be 1030 dry: *The year is dry;* part may be hot: *The year is hot;* part may be mild: *The year is mild.* I attribute to the whole what characterizes a part of it. By this same mode of reckoning, you, Gion, will be accounted turbid and clear, narrow and broad, brackish and sweet, because of some varied part of 1035 your course. Again, by the same figure, a day is to be accounted dry and yet rainy because of a part of it. Since both forms of this figure are pleasing, you may give pleasure by either form.

There is likewise an urbane imprecision of diction when a word is chosen which is neither literal nor precise in its context, but which is related to the literal word. For example, if one 1040 proposes to say: *The strength of the Ithacan is slight, but yet he has a mind of great wisdom,* let catachresis alter the wording thus: *Strength in Ulysses is s h o r t, wisdom in his heart is l o n g,* for there is a certain

7 synecdoche
(*intellectio*)

(a) the part
for the whole

(b) the whole
for the part

8 catachresis
(*abusio*)

1045 affinity between the words *long* and *great*, as between *short* and *slight*.

In the figures given above there is a common element of adornment and weightiness, arising from the fact that an object does not come before us with unveiled face, and accompanied by its natural voice; rather, an alien voice attends it, 1050 and so it shrouds itself in mist, as it were, but in a luminous mist.

9 hyperbaton
(*transgressio*)

A certain weightiness of style results also from the order of words alone, when units grammatically related are separated by their position, so that an

(a) anastrophe
(*perversio*)

inversion of this sort occurs: *rege sub ipso; tempus ad illud; ea de causa; rebus in illis* [under the king himself; up to that time; for this reason; in those

(b) trans-
position
(*transjectio*)

1055 matters]; or a transposed order of this sort: *Dura creavit pestiferam fortuna famem* [harsh fortune produced a pestilent famine]; *Letalis egenam gente fames spoliavit humum* [deadly famine robbed the destitute soil of produce]. Here words related grammatically are separated by their position in the sentence. Juxtaposition of related words conveys the sense more readily, but their moderate separa-
1060 tion sounds better to the ear and has greater elegance.

Obscurity in
tropical figures
is to be avoided

If you wish to speed onward by means of the weighty style, have recourse to these sails, occupy this harbour, cast the mind's anchor here. Yet be weighty in such a manner that your subject is not hidden under a cloud; rather let the words pay 1065 fealty to their rightful lord. Words are instruments to unlock the closed mind; they are keys, as it were, of the mind. One who seeks to open what is closed does not set out to draw a cloud over his words.

If indeed he has done so, he has done an injury
to the words, for he has made a lock out of a key.
Be the bearer of a key, then; open up the subject 1070
readily by your words; for if what is said enters
through the ears into the mind's gaze without light,
it is pouring water into a river, planting in dry soil,
beating in the air, drawing a plow in sterile sand.
If, therefore, you introduce any words that are
strange or recondite, you are displaying your own
virtuosity thereby and not observing the rules of 1075
discourse. The straying tongue must draw back
from this fault and set up barriers against obscure
words. Take counsel: it may be you know all
things — you are greater than others in this —
still, in your mode of expression be one of those
others. Be of average, not lofty, eloquence. The 1080
precept of the ancients is clear: speak as the many,
think as the few. You do not demean yourself by
observing this precept; you can be at once elegant
and easy in discourse. Regard not your own capacities, therefore, but rather his with whom you 1085
are speaking. Give to your words weight suited to
his shoulders, and adapt your speech to the subject.
When you are teaching the arts, let your speech
be native to each art; each delights in its own
idiom. But see that its idiom is kept within its own
borders; when you come out into the common
market-place it is desirable to use the common 1090
idiom. In a common matter, let the style be
common; in specialized matters let the style be
proper to each. Let the distinctive quality of
each subject be respected: in the use of words this
is a very commendable practice.

2. Easy Ornament

The rhetorical
colours   1095

Figures of diction

1 *repetitio*
2 *conversio*
3 *complexio*   1100

4 *traductio* (a)
    (b)

5 *contentio*

6 *exclamatio*   1105

7 *interrogatio*

    1110

8 *ratiocinatio*

    1115

9 *sententia*
10 *contrarium*

11 *membrum*   1120

If a mode of expression both easy and adorned is desired, set aside all the techniques of the dignified style and have recourse to means that are simple, but of a simplicity that does not shock the ear by its rudeness. Here are the rhetorical colours with which to adorn your style:

Deed so evil! Deed more evil than others! Deed most evil of all deeds! O apple! wretched apple! Miserable apple! Why did it affect you, that tasting of Adam? Why do we all weep for the fault of that one man, Adam? That taste of the apple [m ā l i] *was the general cause of evil* [m ă l i]. *The father* [p a t e r], *to us so cruel a foe, showed himself not to be father* [p a t r e m]. *He who was rich became poor; he who was happy, wretched; he who enjoyed such radiance was thrust back into darkness. Where now is Paradise, and that joy of which you were lord? I ask you, most powerful of creatures, whence sprang your great crime? You sin by approving in spirit the deed of your wife, by tasting forbidden fruit, by defending your actions in speech. Approving, tasting, defending, do you not then merit your fall? Tell me, why did you touch fruit so harmful? My wife offered it me. But why did you taste it? She was persuasive. Knowing the deed pernicious, why did you approve? I was afraid of making her angry. After the deed, why were you slow to repent your guilt by petitioning God for pardon? Say, in this deed of death, what reason was found? There was only delusion for reason.*

He is free who is not a slave to vice. But since that man was a slave, shall we enjoy freedom? If he who was strong in great virtue did not resist the foe, how shall we who are frail resist? The fall began with the enemy,

and by his cunning we fell, and corrupt as we are we
cannot live without falling. Of avail to the fallen is aid   12 *articulus*
of this kind: tears, fasting, psalms.

The unclean spirit does not harm him for whom God   13 *continuatio*
is more powerful than the world. He who places no hope in   1125 — in *sententia*
the foe — whence can he fear the foe? If the foe is wont   — in *contrario*
to be grievously harmful only to those who are his, bene-   — in *occlusione*
volent law does not suffer us to be of his tribe. Lest
perchance tempests by their violence overwhelm us, let us   14 *compar*
preserve honour and reject evil. For virtue is most ex-   1130
cellent [o p t i m a] of all things, vice [v i t i u m] is   15 *similiter*
the worst [p e s s i m a] of things — nothing is so per-   *cadens*
nicious [p e r n i c i o s u m].

This he had proved [e x p e r t u s], this he pitied   16 *similiter*
[m i s e r t u s] — he who, deigning to be born [n a s c i],   *desinens*
came to be reborn [r e n a s c i] from death; the man who
could be [p o t u i t] — he alone — the being who brought
good [p r o f u i t] to all. Here in flesh [c a r n e]   17 *adnominatio*
without flaw [c a r i e], not caught in fault's [c r i m i-   1135
n i s] net [h a m o], a man [h o m o] simple and suppliant
[s i m p l e x, s u p p l e x], he set at naught [l u s i t], the
insidious serpent who deceived us [e l u s i t], and, made a
hostage [h o s t i a], he destroyed the hostile one [h o s-
t e m] and by his dying dismayed him [m o r i e n d o,
r e m o r d i t].

Serpent of envy and foe of our race, why did you seek   18 *subjectio*
Christ's death on the cross? Did he deserve it? But he   1140
was free of all guilt. Did you think his body a phantom?
But he assumed true flesh of a virgin. Did you think
him mere man? But by his power he proved himself God.
Deservedly, therefore, are you condemned. Remember,
the servant who condemns his master will be condemned   1145
by him. So condemnation justly came to a close with him
from whom it began. For the enemy had first condemned   19 *gradatio*

*Eve; Eve, secondly, condemned her husband; her husband,
thirdly, condemned all his offspring; the offspring,
fourthly, condemned God; God, last of all, condemned the*
1150 *enemy whose cause of death he was — he was, and so
to the world he brought good; he brought good, and it was
made free; it was made free because he redeemed all
things. If he contended by his own power and effortlessly,*

20 *definitio*   *he would have saved all things. For his might is a virtue
almighty, and his is the power to do all things by a nod*

21 *transitio*   1155 *or a word or simply by willing. You see that he could do
this; in the sequel you will hear why this was not his will.
Here is his reasoning: if open violence were offered the*

22 *correctio*   *foe, God could be — nay, would be — not acting in
accord with strict justice in this. The demands of justice*

23 *occupatio*   *decreed — but I pass this by as well known — that as the*
1160 *enemy brought death to mankind through treacherous
means, so man by subtle maneuver should bring death
to the enemy, taken captive in the toils of divinity. For*

24 *disjunctio*   *this reason, to dwell with us in true flesh God came;
marked with the stain of our flesh he could not be; and at*
1165 *length those who were his in his own blood he washed.*

25 *conjunctio*   *Lord of life and death as he was, death he rent asunder and*
26 *adjunctio* (a) *life — rent life asunder by dying, and death by rising*
   (b)   *again; not by the life he first assumed, but by that same
life resumed his own he redeemed.*

27 *conduplicatio*   *Betrayer of human nature — betrayer, I say, where is*
1170 *now your strength ? Where is your strength ? Death has
broken your bonds; his death with wondrous power has
broken your bonds. Death how happy ! How happy a*

28 *interpretatio*   *death ! That death our redemption ! This death of his
healed the wounds of our soul; washed the unclean;*

29 *commutatio*   *removed guilt. O how holy the grace of Christ ! How*
30 *permissio*   1175 *gracious the holiness ! To you, fount of holiness, I
wholly dedicate myself from this time. Confer, take*

away; scourge, spare; command, forbid; do whichever you
wish; lo, I am your servant, Lord; use your servant just as
you please; whatever you do, I give thanks. O Jesus so
good, what shall I call you ? If I call you holy, or holiness 1180   **31** *dubitatio*
itself, or fountain of holiness, or add still more, you are
greater yet. This being so great willed to become so small.
Coming in the form of a servant, he came to recover the
sheep he had lost, sheep which would be snatched by
violence from the enemy, not by judgement, unless perchance 1185
he defeated the foe just as man had before been defeated.
But such a one had to be a pure man, or an angel, or God.   **32** *expeditio*
A pure man he could not be, for pure man straightway
was impure and could easily fall into sin. Angel you
could not be, for since the angelic nature had fallen you 1190
would not stand firm in ours. Yet let it be so ! Let it be
granted that one or the other had stood strong in virtue
and wrought our redemption. To be created is certainly
less than to be redeemed. Redeemed man would be less
bound, then, to the creator and more to him who redeemed; 1195
and so there would have been need of one greater than his
creator. It was necessary, therefore, that God become man
— God whose fullness of wisdom controlled human faculties
with the reins of divinity. To him alone the world owed
both its creation and its redemption; and to God alone it 1200
gave worship. As the need had directed, so was its ful-   **33** *dissolutio*
filment in act. For other persons there remains a single
nature; the Son united himself to ours, enclosed in the
womb of a virgin. Her womb enclosed him whom the
world could not contain; he had a beginning in time who 1205
existed before time was. True man, true God, he ex-
perienced all that is proper to us, sin only excepted. En-
during mockery, he was silent; beaten with stripes, he
passed thurogh the bonds of death; his gentle body hung
on the fearful cross; his spirit, sent forth, came as rare 1210

guest to the realms below; after three days he returned to life, victorious by his own power. Thus the shepherd led back to the fold the sheep that had been drawn astray.

34 *praecisio*   *How great an event was this! And what... but I let the word pass, for no word can be found adequate to so great*

35 *conclusio*   1215 *a marvel. Therefore since they could not be redeemed unless God was made man, and unless, once made man, he determined to conquer death, the conquering of death redeemed those who were his from death.*

The exercise given above has gathered together the flowers of diction; in these figures there is both easy intelligibility and a literal use of words. No 1220 figure is missing from the number, and the usual order of the colours is retained. If occasionally I have given words a metaphorical sense, it has been in accord with good taste to combine difficult ornaments with easy so that the easy style, although it affords pleasure by the sweetness of its own manner, might give still greater pleasure if seasoned with the flavour of difficult figures. In this way, then, 1225 let the mind's finger pluck its blooms in the field of rhetoric. But see that your style blossoms sparingly with such figures, and with a variety, not a cluster of the same kind. From varied flowers a sweeter fragrance rises; faulty excess renders insipid what is full of flavour.

Figures of   1230   There are other figures to adorn the meaning of
thought   words. All of these I include in the following brief treatment: when meaning is adorned, this is the

1 *distributio*   standard procedure. *Distributio* assigns specific roles to various things or among various persons.

2 *licentia*   1235 At times, *licentia*, fairly and lawfully, chides masters or friends, offending no one with its words. At

3 *diminutio*   times, *diminutio* implies more in the subject than is

expressed in words, and makes its point by understatement, though with moderation. So, too,
descriptio presents consequences, and the eventualities
that can ensue from a given situation. It gives a
full and lucid account with a certain dignity of
presentation. Or again, *disjunctio* distinguishes
alternatives, accompanying each with a reason,
and bringing both to a conclusion. Or single
details are brought together, and *frequentatio* gathers
up points that had been scattered through the
work. By turning a subject over repeatedly and
varying the figure, I seem to be saying a number of
things whereas I am actually dwelling on one
thing, in order to give it a finer polish and impart
a smooth finish by repeated applications of the
file, one might say. This is done in two ways:
either by saying the same thing with variations,
or by elaborating upon the same thing. We may
say the same thing with variations in three ways;
we may elaborate upon the same thing with variations in seven ways. You may read about all of
these at greater length in Cicero. [By *commoratio*]
I go deeply into one point and linger on in the
same place; or [by *contentio*] I institute a comparison
in which the positions set forth are antithetical
to each other. Often from an object basically
dissimilar I draw forth a point of resemblance. Or
I present as exemplum, with the name of a definite
authority, some statement he has made or some
deed he has performed. Or I pass over the figures
just mentioned, and, as another figure comes to
the fore, I introduce a comparison of one thing
with a similar thing by means of an appropriate
image. Or there is a figure allied to this last one,

4 *descriptio*

1240

5 *disjunctio*

6 *frequentatio*

7 *expolitio*

1245

1250

8 *commoratio*

9 *contentio*

10 *similitudo*

1255

11 *exemplum*

12 *imago*

1260

13 *effictio*

14 *notatio*

15 *sermocinatio* 1265

16 *conformatio*

17 *significatio* 1270

18 *brevitas*

19 *demonstratio*

1275

whereby I depict or represent corporeal appearance, in so far as is requisite. Again, I set down certain distinguishing marks — very definite signs, as it were — by which I describe clearly the character of a man; this is a better and more effective figure. There is another figure whereby a speech is adapted to the person speaking, and what is said gives the very tone and manner of the speaker. Again, adorning the subject with a different kind of freshness, at one time I fashion a new person by giving the power of speech where nature has denied it; at another, I leave to suspicion more than I actually put into words; again, I compress the entire subject into a few words — those which are essential to it and no others. At another time the subject is revealed so vividly that it seems to be present to the eyes; this effect will be perfectly achieved by five means: if I show what precedes, what constitutes, and what follows the event itself, what circumstances attend it, and what consequences follow upon it.

You may read, in the passage given above, the list of figures of thought, their number (twice ten, if you subtract one), and the sequence they observe. Since the order I followed above will not be varied, I have rendered the subject clear by offering examples.

1 *distributio* 1280
(distribution)

2 *licentia*
(frankness)

3 *diminutio* 1285
(understatement)

To proclaim sacred laws is the pope's prerogative; to observe the form of law prescribed is the part of lesser men. But very many go astray, and that straying judges you, holy Father. You spare, and do not punish, those who seek shameful gain. They buy and sell what is illicit, with no one to avenge their guilt. Powerful Father, you whose power is by no means brief, be mindful of

*vengeance. Gentle Father, unsheathe at some time the
sword's point. If vengeance sleeps, the guilty will range
like a wolf crouched to spring, or a fox lurking in wait
for the doe. In one place he will bring to completion, in
another he will meditate crimes; in one instance under
cover, in another out in the open, replete with malice in* 1290
*both. His evils are two: the fraud of simony, the coldness
of avarice. He embraces both the one and the other, and
does not abhor them. But I labour with futile voice;
whatever I may say against him, I am washing brick.
If I give my approval, that is not what he deserves; if I* 1295
*condemn, his crime does not move him. Note what bitter
poison he bears: he will be seen as a flatterer face to face,
a detractor when out of sight; an apparent friend, a
secret enemy; an avaricious owner, a cruel extortioner;
an oppressive plunderer, an ingratiating huckster; an
illicit buyer, swift to the evil of simony, now so common.* 1300
*Most excellent Father, avenger of crimes, extend your
hand to destroy this evil. The wisdom of the pope wishes
to suppress what is wicked, and it is his duty to do so.
Neither the task nor the will is alien to a prudent pope.
As a good pope, ponder thus in your heart very often:* 1305
*"O how marvelous the virtue of God! How mighty his
power! How great I now am! How insignificant I
once was! From a small stock I have grown in a trice to a
mighty cedar. He who is God of gods has magnified his
own work; he has willed me in the flower of youth to be
the head of old men. O wonderful gift! He gives to a* 1310
*young man the keys of the heavenly kingdom and authority
over the world. Not much time has passed since my heart
was a novice in knowledge; my speech was unpolished, my
power slight. Now he has so raised up my heart and my
lips and my power, and so placed them in this office above* 1315
others, that I am the world's sole wonder. This is not

4 *descriptio*
(description)

5 *disjunctio*
(division)

6 *frequentatio*
(accumulation)

7 *expolitio*
(refining)
— by verbal changes

— by dialogue
(*per sermocinationem*)

the doing of man; the grace of the Highest has set me highest; no praise is due me in this, but thanks is due him from whose fullness we have received all things. Hence I am bound more firmly, and more strictly obliged to him 1320 *to put down what he wills to put down, to raise up what he wills to raise, to wish what he wishes, to hate what he hates. And I desire to be so bound; and I will put down all he has ordered put down, I will raise what he ordered raised, solicitous for one thing alone: to will what he*

— by arousal 1325 *wills, to hate what he hates". Who is so void of wit, so* (*per exsuscitationem*) *destitute of soul, so distracted, that he would not praise this work, that he would not judge it to be the work of a*

(i) theme stated *prudent nature? So a prudent pope bases all his efforts* with reason added *on this, and because of this, that such great power has accrued to him for this end: to take away the sins of the* 1330 *world, to make the world clean, in order to lead it by the*

(ii) theme re-stated *straight path to heaven. Since God has raised him up for* with reason *this work, it is his concern to accomplish the task allotted.*

(iii) theme re-stated without reasons *Therefore if he is remiss in this, he is fountain and source of two wrongs: for he is his own enemy and the*

(iv) argument 1335 *public enemy as well. Is it better to injure the world by* from the contrary *torpid sleep than to promote its interests by vigilant care?*

(v) with a comparison *Take heed and remember: the pope like a good shepherd guards his fold from the jaws of the wolf; or, as a physician cures bodies, so he, as physician and shepherd, heals*

(vi) with an 1340 *souls and their wounds. Our God, making all things* exemplum *whole, laid down his life for his sheep. So it is evident, by force of both reason and example, that the sins of the*

(vii) closing the *world must be taken away. Suppress wickedness, then,* argument *holy Father, successor of Peter; and with his Simon*

[8 *commoratio*] *let simony be brought to destruction. His own sordid gain* 9 *contentio* 1345 *gratifies each man; the general depravity oppresses you* (antithesis) *only. This one sin is corrupting all men. It may be that no mortal thing disturbs them, yet while this stands against*

them the death of the soul results from one sin as well as
from many: just as a ship is engulfed in the rising seas
because of one crack no less than of many — both dangers 1350
have the same destructive effect. Yet it can hardly be that
a man may live without fault, whence Cato the moralist
says: "No one lives without fault." That spirit of
nature malign, the general foe, swoops round man on 1355
hidden wings, with tortured desire to win back the one
whom he lost. That great champion of ours snatched
man away with the mighty power of a lion, the cunning
of a serpent, and the simplicity of a dove. Who is he?
He is, indeed, of two natures. Free of all blemish,
somewhat ruddy of countenance, pleasant to view, paragon 1360
of angels, a form beautiful above the forms of men,
special image of the Father; he, the second Adam, who
opened for us the gates of life with the key of his death.
Called as we are to those joys, what do we do? We are 1365
apathetic, in the image of the lazy man. Do you know the
procrastination of the lazy man? If he is called in the
morning he refuses to hear. If he is summoned repeatedly,
with insistent voice, he snores loudly through his nose,
although he is awake. Forced at length by the shouts,
but sluggish of speech, he gets his tongue moving and
"What do you want with me," he says. — "Get up!
Come on now!" — "It's night, let me sleep." "No, 1370
it's daytime; get up!" — "Ye gods! Look — I am
getting up. Go ahead; I'll be there." But he doesn't follow
the man he's fooling; and then: "Aren't you coming?"
"I'd have been there by now, but I'm looking for my
clothes and can't find them." — "It's no use — I know
you, Birria. Get up at once!" — "Sir, I'm right with 1375
you." But he isn't; rather he turns his head to this side
and that, or scratches his arms, or stretches his limbs.
So he looks for any excuse for delay. With his lips, he is

10 *similitudo*
(comparison)

11 *exemplum*

12 *imago*
(image
or simile)

13 *effictio*
(portrayal)

14 *notatio*
(character
delineation)

always coming — but not with his feet. So, coming, he
1380 *never arrives — not he. Driven to it, perhaps, he drags*
his steps as he moves, matching a turtle's pace. We, when
called to true joys, are the very image of this man. En-
chanted by pleasures of many kinds, we close up the ears of
our heart; or, if our ears are open, we still put off coming
to those joys. Or if we come, unwillingly drawn perhaps,
1385 *we move at the pace of a tortoise. Reckless of our welfare,*
we neglect our Lord for the foe. Ah wretched men! Why
will we not remember the day of counsel, on which his
hand redeemed us from the claws of the enemy; remember,
indeed, what things he endured, what manner of things, what
1390 *great things, in torments, in mocking words? The servant*

15 *sermocinatio*
(dialogue)

of the high priest maliciously denounced the replies of our
Lord, and striking him said: "Do you answer the high
priest thus?" He gently responded: "Friend, if I have
spoken anything ill, tell me in what. If well, why do you
1395 *strike me?". To you also, Pilate, resisting as far as*
you could, Judea thundered, howling "Crucify him!" —
taking up the cry and roaring again, "Crucify him!"
As they struck him with blows, another added these
mocking words: "Prophesy, Christ, who is it that struck
1400 *you"? Insolently another continued: "Others he saved,*
in his own cause he's a failure. He hoped in the Lord, let
the Lord, if he wills, release him". He willed to be
treated thus with contempt, he who was scourged with
rods, hung on the wood of the cross, given vinegar to
drink, pierced with a lance, struck with a reed, his head
1405 *crowned with sharp thorns; enduring all sorrows, he*
ended deaths so varied in one death. [Spittle, the lash,
threats, reproaches, nails, the lance, thorns — in his
blessed death, these are the goal to which our fall led.
By these delights, O man, by this craft of the cross, he
1410 *redeemed you, strongly weak while he destroyed death*

by dying]. *When he suffered death, nature said: "I*   16 *conformatio*
must needs suffer; my Lord is suffering. Lament with   (personification)
me, all manner of things; heaven, hide your lights;
grow darkling, O air; seas, roar aloud; tremble, O earth;
all elements weep together." Nature shuddered in lamen- 1415
tation and was rent apart wholly. All manner of things gave
forth signs: heaven hiding her lights, the air growing dark,
the sea roaring aloud, earth trembling, all the elements in
tears. That did not happen in accord with the natural 1420
sequence of things, but because the Lord of nature had
suffered the violence of death. Nature suffered that
violence with you, compelled by your sorrow. Only a
people perverse scoffed at the dying God; their subsequent   17 *significatio*
history bears the shame. Treacherous race! Stiff-necked   (implication,
generation! Learn to soften that heart so hardened; 1425   emphasis)
remember the fearful destruction of cruel Pharaoh. Learn
how to be blessed; search out each detail about Christ; you
will see with clear eyes. Ought not Christ to have suffered
thus? According to the inscription there written, the Lord
reigned from the cross and won there the victory, repelled 1430
the enemy and redeemed the world. Thus a man fought   18 *brevitas*
for mankind, but that man was God; a combatant then,   (conciseness)
now wielding a royal sceptre, and, in time to come, judge.
That the saviour of man had to be God and no other, the   19 *demonstratio*
Son, not the Father or Holy Spirit, conclude from these 1435   (vivid de-
few remarks. When the angelic choirs were created at   monstration)
heaven's birth, Lucifer, peerless in radiance, drew from
the creator's radiance more light than others; therefore he — before the event
grew presumptuous. Then, swelling with pride, he
began to aspire towards the ultimate light. For he saw 1440
Light begotten of Light, the Word of the Father; he saw,
too, the Holy Spirit proceeding from both; he saw the
same nature in all three; he saw they were three distinct
persons. He envied the one sole Word, and he who was 1445

creature wished to be equal to the one begotten of the
Father: "I propose to settle in the regions of the north,"
he said, "and to seem like to the most high." Thus he
willed sin to become an inhabitant of heaven; but its
residence was brief, for heaven could not endure what was
1450 sinful. Lucifer straightway fell there as he had risen,
and his dawn was swiftly changed into dusk, his goodness
to evil, his apex to nadir; saint became demon. He had
been of two forms in one hour: bright and dark, good and
1455 evil, high and lowest, angel and devil. He who suffered
that fall dragged down to the depths a tenth part of all
the angelic orders and brought on each one alike its own
ruin. After a space of five days, the sixth day fashioned
Adam; it formed Eve as well — citizens of your realm,
1460 Paradise. To them their creator said: "Taste every kind
of fruit, both of good and of evil; touch not the tree of
knowledge." Moreover, he added the cause: lest by
tasting they die the death. And what of Satan? He
saw them, saw them fashioned for this purpose: to make
up the number of the angelic host that had fallen, and to
1465 enjoy those delights which the angel lost. Then, pondering
what he might do, taking the form of a serpent, advancing
straight and erect, he came in secret to Eve, not daring to
speak to Adam: "Why," he said, "are you forbidden to
eat of that tree which was mentioned?" She replied,
1470 "For this reason, indeed: lest perchance through it we die."
At that "perchance" he saw her unstable in faith; and
then, gaining assurance, he overcame her with this:
"Not so," he said, "on the contrary, eat; and thus you
can be, as the gods are, expert in good and evil." Vain
1475 hope of a promise so great puffed her up; she tasted what
was forbidden; and her husband, lest he distress her —
although with full knowledge — did likewise. That was
— after the event   the primal sin; but their second fault was more grievous:

to be unwilling to repent their guilt and implore God's
pardon by prayer. Indeed, he even cast the crime back on
his wife's initiative. And what of the wife? She in 1480
turn cast it back on the serpent's guile. This defense of
their guilt was the source of a greater offense. Thus they
fell from your throne, Paradise, each one condemned.
So the human race perished. Neither natural nor legal 1485
right, nor power of any kind, was of avail to the race to
prevent Tartarus from swallowing all souls. Great
was the wrath that thundered as so many thousands of
years rolled by, and still the fierce storm was not quelled.
Therefore the Son of God pondered: "Because Lucifer   — the attendant
presumed against me, he fell and was lost. That fall of 1490   circumstances
his was the root of this one. So I am, as it were, a remote
cause of this plight: I shall be the cause of a kindred
salvation. If I choose to contend by my own strength,
the enemy will easily fall. But if I conquer in that way,
I shall be using strength and not judgement. Therefore
since the cunning of the enemy overcame man, it follows 1495
necessarily, by the order of reason, that it should be man
who overcomes him; that he who slipped and fell should
rise up and strongly tear himself free from the claws of
Satan; that he who bore the yoke of a slave should walk 1500
freely with head erect; that he who perished in misery
should live on in joy. But that man must be God: only
if God assumed flesh would man's power overthrow his
enemy, for thus human power became one with the power
of God. It is therefore necessary that, as the enemy hurled 1505
man down, he be hurled down by man; as he overcame by
means of a tree, so by a tree he be overcome; that he be
taken in the very snare which he laid." So spoke the Son.
The Paraclete was author of his conception, and with
his own hand fashioned human attire for the one who 1510
descended in secret into a virgin's womb through closed

gates; and went forth from that virgin's womb, again through closed gates. A marvelous thing every way: marvelous the ingress, marvelous the egress, and marvelous the whole progress of his life. In him the enemy found — aspects of 1515 *nothing to claim as his own. Yet he attacked a being not* the event itself *his; condemning him, condemned by him, he condemned him to the death of the cross. He bore our sins on the cross, not his own. He washed away our crimes there; and discharged a debt he had not incurred. But death* 1520 *itself did not evade him when it thus invaded his life. When it would swallow the man, it was intercepted by the hook of his divinity; and so it thought to defeat what it swallowed, but was struck aghast to be defeated, for* — its consequences *his spirit robbed Tartarus of its due, and transformed* 1525 *the darkness of grief into raptures of light for his friends. Those whom the region of death held, his grace alone thus redeemed; so wrath was at an end, because of him on whose account it began.*

Varieties of *significatio*

1 understatement

2 hyperbole

If you examine these rhetorical figures carefully, in all of them the meaning clearly reveals its 1530 content. You will find only two where it does not present the content in a readily apparent manner.

If this statement is proposed: *My power is not slight, my dignity not insignificant,* I am implying more than I say, and the actual situation is of greater consequence than the words indicate. If I happen to be speaking on behalf of my friends, or on my own behalf, this manner of speech is in good 1535 taste, and I show becoming modesty in employing such an expression. In this way, the meaning makes its appearance veiled; the true situation is not clearly apparent; there is more consequence in the actual fact than the expression of it indicates.

From the numerous and great resources left by his

father, the squanderer of wealth has not enough to conceal his poverty with a covering, nor even an earthen jug in 1540 *which to beg a fire.* Here I speak in excessive terms about a thing that is in itself excessive; I chide immoderately what is not moderate; there is moderation neither in the actual situation nor in my expression of it. If the situation is more moderate than my words, still the excessive language does suggest that there is less excess in the fact itself.

That peerless man: the word means *most excellent;* 1545 but *most vicious* glances at us obliquely: this is its meaning. The word belies its appearance, or else our perception errs. In such ambiguities, the actual fact is veiled and the mockery is obvious.

3 ambiguity

The boy's ruddy colour fled his cheeks when he saw the rods, and his countenance was bloodless. Such pallor 1550 indicates that he was afraid. *A blush had spread over the maiden's face;* her appearance indicates that she was ashamed. *The stroller went sauntering on with hair adorned*; the manner of expression suggests dissolute conduct. Note the signs that accompany a given circumstance. Present the facts, but do not 1555 present them as such; rather, reveal only signs of the facts: show fear by pallor, sensuality by adornment, and shame by a sudden blush; show the thing itself by its definite signs, what is prior by what is consequent upon it: this complexion, this sex, this age, that form.

4 consequence

Recently in another's chamber... but I will not say it. 1560 In this way I break off my words, and I do not say *that man*, but *a man of such-and-such an age*, or *of a certain appearance.*

5 aposiopesis

You are great, and the world supplicates you on bent knee. Although you have power to vent your rage, do not

6 analogy

1565 *do so; remember Nero.* After introducing an analogy
in this way, I add nothing further. Or here I
offer a different example contained in the following
story:

When Alexander the Great declared war on Athens,
no terms for restoration of peace were acceptable unless
perchance the sages of the city were surrendered as pledge.
1570 *One of the wise men replied to the proposal in these words:*
"It happened that a wolf declared war on a shepherd.
Terms of peace were discussed between them, but no
covenant of peace was agreeable to the wolf unless as
pledge and warrant of amity the guardian of the flock
was handed over to him. When this was done, the enemy
1575 *who before had been cautious then became more assured."*
After saying this much, he ceased.

He did not wish to apply the analogy between
the proposal and the exemplum, for he wisely gave
part to the ears and left part to the understanding.
This is the method of a skilled speaker, to include
the whole force of a remark in half a remark.

1580 Thought, finding excellent adornment in such
devices, does not appear unveiled, but makes itself
known by signs. It shines with an oblique ray and
chooses not to advance directly into the light.
There are five species [of *significatio*], but all are
forms of the same device.

Bring together flowers of diction and thought,
1585 that the field of discourse may blossom with both
sorts of flowers, for a mingled fragrance, blending
adornment of both kinds, rises and spreads its
sweetness.

3. *Theory of Conversions*

You know what is fitting, and you say the fitting
thing, yet you may be guided by chance, not

by a principle of art. You do not understand what
to look for in a subject at first glance, and on what 1590
aspect to concentrate your attention; at what point
you should begin applying your efforts, and what
source gives rise to the adornment of words. Your
mind wanders over one part after another, and
your aimless steps betray a mind unsure of itself,
like the steps of a blind man feeling out where or 1595
what his way is — one whose staff is his eye and
whose guide is fortune. What then ? By the precepts
of art you may curb your mind so it will not wander
like a buffoon. Begin at a definite place. There
are only three places: first, a word inflected by
tense; secondly, a word inflected by case; finally, 1600
a word that remains unchanged. The method of
approach is as follows.

Let us take the first place: consider the verb.
Change it into a noun — one which derives from
that same verb, or from one synonymous with it,
or from one similar to it by reason of some obvious 1605
likeness. A noun derives from its verb as a branch
grows from its trunk and retains the life of its root.
Now, since the noun does this, and is not itself
sufficient for our purpose, the fire as a whole will
be built up from this spark by the keen discernment 1610
of the mind as it adds other words. Maneuver the
subject about in this way, concentrating intently
upon it: change the noun about into any case at
all, and adapt to it, in each of its cases, a related
series of words which may adequately express the
proposed statement. To this end, you will struggle
with the whole force of your mind. Hammer it
out with a will on the forge of the understanding, 1615
pound it again and again, and at last pound out

(1) The verb : its
conversion into one
or more nouns

what is suitable. Now, the method of procedure is this: first, bring together in your mind all the grammatical forms; next, choose the most effective one — that case through which meaning enters the ear most delightfully. A discerning judge must
1620 be at work here; he must see with discernment. To be discerning, you need both theory and practice. Precept may be clarified here by example; take the following brief theme: *I am grieving over this matter.* Now apply the principle just established: *From this fountain grief flows over me. Hence the*
1625 *root (or the seed, or the fount, or the source) of grief rises within me. This affair is matter and cause for grief. It sows (or gives birth to, or piles up) grief. With cruel wounds, tormenting grief, you rage against me. My mind, as it were, lies prostrate, injured and ill*
1630 *with grief.* So, from the verb *grieve,* take the noun *grief;* change it around into any case; add to it, in whatever case it may be, a related sequence of words to suit the subject. Or, again, take a noun not from that same verb, but from a similar verb
1635 suggesting grief — for example: *sigh, complain, groan, weep.* The nouns from these verbs are: *tears, groans, sighs, complaints.* Nouns, in this way, express the force of the verbs: *Sighs rise from my soul, complaints from my lips; tears flow down my cheeks;*
1640 *I utter continual groans.* Now say it more elegantly thus: *Sighs break forth from the depths of my heart; heaven rings with my complaints; the fount of my eyes floods forth tears; groans rend asunder my spirit.* Metaphor, in this way, binds nouns to verbs with, one might say, the knot of artistic skill.
1645 Grace of expression is, indeed, pleasant when words are used literally, but the accompanying pleasure

is greater when they are skilfully converted to metaphor.

A word inflected by case may follow two methods: one is valid for an adjective, the other for a noun. You study one apart from the other, but in this present formulation consider the adjective first. *(2) Declinable words* *1650*

The directive given above for the conversion of a verb is valid in an analogous way for the conversion of an adjective. Proceed by the same steps here as you did there, for the two paths follow the same route. This is clearly evident in the following example: *Her countenance is r a d i a n t.* Change the adjective, observing the rule given above: *R a-d i a n c e brightens her countenance. It glows with the beam (or with the light) o f r a d i a n c e. Her visage is wedded t o r a d i a n c e. Her chin wears a r a-d i a n c e like the sun's. Dawn breaks on the world f r o m t h e r a d i a n c e of her cheek alone.* This is an effective method; when employed with hyperbole it intensifies or diminishes eulogy or denunciation to a marked degree. Denunciation and panegyric offer suitable occasions for this technique. Thus you will take *radiance* from *radiant*, to find a more effective means of expression by trying the various cases. Or again, take a noun not from the adjective *radiant* but from one that resembles it: *snowy;* and, deriving a noun from the adjective — that is, *snow* — follow this sequence: *S n o w and her cheek are not remote in beauty. Radiance glows in her face with a light as intense as if it were rival o f s n o w. Her features in their radiance are likened t o s n o w. In its natural brilliance her visage resembled the s n o w. Confident of victory, her features* *(a) the adjective: its conversion into one or more nouns* *1655* *1660* *1665* *1670 contend w i t h   t h e   s n o w.* I am omitting the fifth case, which is to be used when apostrophe requires it.

1675 In the way just described, you may change an adjective into a noun derived from it, or from another adjective like it; and the skilful writer will devise other words, giving elegance to their grouping, so that the combination of words added to the noun will retain the meaning of the original statement while varying the rhetorical colour; and will say the same thing without sounding the same.

1680 For a noun, follow this process: if the noun is appropriate as it stands, it does not need the craftsman's attention. If it is not appropriate in its present case, change it from case to case, and try to weave together a texture of words in such a way that a plain statement assumes a robe of novelty 1685 and beauty. Here is the unadorned face of a theme: *I have done the evil deed o n   p u r p o s e.* Now I give freshness to the face of the word: *My p u r- p o s e was the spur to action,* or: *was instigator of the evil deed.* Or: *The prompting o f   a   v i c i o u s   p u r- p o s e offered itself* or *came forward as an argument for* 1690 *crime.* Or try the word in this case: *The deed was in accord w i t h   t h e   p u r p o s e,* or *A villainous hand was accomplice t o   t h e   p u r p o s e.* Or suggest a wording like this: *A criminal hand extended p u r- p o s e to action.* Again, if anyone should offer you this "raw" statement, so to speak: *Everyone talks* 1695 *of this d e e d,* dress the word thus: *This d e e d is the cry of the people;* or: *Common gossip is witness o f t h e   d e e d;* or: *No tongue gives the nay t o t h e d e e d, but the people's voice, one and all, proclaims it.*

(b) the noun : conversion of cases and finding of new nouns

Shall I offer further examples ? To what end ?
Meaning rejects no grammatical case; one and 1700
the same meaning may be adjusted to all cases.
Cultivate an ability to find the way: it lies open to
discovery, if only you are able to discover it. If
the way is not clear to anyone, that is not the way's
fault, but his who lacks an understanding of art
and has no skilled colleague to consult. Three
things perfect a work: artistic theory by whose law 1705
you may be guided; experience, which you may
foster by practice; and superior writers, whom you
may imitate. Theory makes the craftsman sure;
experience makes him ready; imitation makes him
versatile; the three together produce the greatest
craftsmen.

The unchanging array of words which do not
admit of inflection, although permissible in dis- 1710
course, are well set aside. Their tribe will often,
and preferably, withdraw from the hall, to be
presented under some different form. The new
form should be this: see what such a word signifies,
then express by a noun or a verb the concept
signified, so that a new verbal structure results,
more effective than the original one. Take this 1715
brief theme: *T h e n he will come. Then* is a sign of
time. Express that time by a noun, while preserving
the same general meaning: *T h a t   d a y will bring
him.* If this is your theme: *He will come h i t h e r,*
the following expression will add grace to your
words: *T h i s   p l a c e will welcome his coming, o r* 1720
will be host to his arrival, host of a year or a day. If you
prefer a more ornate style, elaborate on the theme.
If you intend to say: *Once (o r twice, o r frequently)
I am at fault,* say rather: *This is the sole (o r second,*

(3) Uninflecter
words : theid
conversion
into nouns
and verbs

1725 *or habitual) transgression of my spirit;* or: *Felony takes
its rise (or returns, or grows habitual) within me.*
Follow the same directive when *iste* or *ille, alter*
and *alteruter* are used (if the disjunction is minor,
use *alteruter;* if it is definite, use *alter*). Do not
1730 introduce a remark of this kind: *If that man [i l l e]
comes, this one [i s t e] will depart.* Say rather: *That
man [i l l e] will make his arrival the occasion of this
one's [i s t i u s] departure.* The former wording was
the manner of inexperience; the second, the manner
of art. Here is another instance of the same sort:
*The people run c o m p l e t e l y around the city —
the people round the city's circuit on swift foot. He is
1735 j u s t l y punished for his crime — his crime is the
ample reason for his punishment.*

Lest examples weary anyone, I include many
under a few, and the others under these I have
given. If you wish to know the force of more
numerous examples, consider a few; the many are
as the few. Study these few; the law that holds
1740 good for them holds good for the greater number.
The author adds in the *Topics*: by gazing at fewer
things we make greater progress. Lest I meander
in lengthy examples, let many points, by a sounder
principle, be covered in a single brief illustration:
1745 You are an annoying debt-collector; your refrain
is: *You're trying to hold out.* [My reply:] *You want
things on the dot. I need time; I have to think my way
through. You're too persistent a dun. I can't make it
today. Be patient. Tomorrow can do what today cannot.*

This skill does not come easily and without
1750 effort; but when the mind concentrates upon it,
it is as eager as a wrestler to enter the combat. Its

struggle, indeed, is with itself. It seeks its own counsel and does not find it. It tries again, and is rebuffed a second time. It presses on with greater energy, and yet continues to resist itself. Tormented by its labours, it is in anguish; and at last, by violent effort, it wrings out from itself what it wishes. So 1755 it exults, victor over itself and self-vanquished. If you wish to enjoy this happy victory, amplify what is slight, prune what is redundant, groom what is shaggy, clarify what is obscure, correct what is faulty. Every aspect of the work will be 1760 sound because of your careful efforts.

4. Theory of Determinations

Add this to the precepts above: since a word that is uttered alone is, as it were, the raw material of discourse — a thing rough and shapeless, so to speak — give it a companion. This addition will confer shapeliness.

Let metaphor grace the period to brighten its charm, when two words join in a partnership like 1765 this: *the meadow smiles*, or *study flowers*. Or join closely related words, several pairs of them, in a series of this sort: *There appeared, to the table's disgrace, a soiled covering, bran bread, rough food, bitter drink, a slatternly attendant.* Or we may double the 1770 adjective thus: *The table was poor and small, its covering old and threadbare, the food poorly cooked and rough, the drink sour and brackish, the table's attendant gross and awkward. The whole was utterly lacking in grace.* Or a noun may determine another noun, 1775 in this way: *You are Cato in intelligence, Tully in eloquence, Paris in beauty, Pyrrhus in strength.* Again, you may employ the second noun as metaphor, thus:

Determination of a noun

— by a verb

— by a single adjective

— by more than one adjective

— by another noun

the rose of her countenance, the lily of her brow, the ivory of her teeth, the fire of her lips, the balsam of her breath. Or again, in a figurative but commendable
1780 style, say: *Love's Tiphys, Samson's Delila, Cato's Martia.*

Determination of an adjective by a noun

A noun may determine an adjective in much the same way as it determines another noun. Thus a noun in the genitive case may determine an ad-

— in the genitive

jective: if, for instance, in the following words a
1785 miser is said to be *full o f r i c h e s, empty o f v i r t u e s, most avid o f p o s s e s s i o n s, prodigal o f a n o t h e r' s p r o p e r t y, sparing and retentive of*

— in the dative

his own. Or a noun in the dative case may determine an adjective — as here, if I am describing Nero: *His mind is detestable f o r i t s m a n y v i c e s, formed hostile t o s t r a n g e r s, worse still t o h i s f o l l o w e r s, worst of all t o h i m s e l f, helpful*
1790 *t o n o o n e, destructive t o a l l.* Or here are the

— in other cases

other cases: *Disgusting i n a l l h i s c o n v e r s a t i o n at table, always ready w i t h a v i d g l u t t o n y f o r e x c e s s, not approving the wines unless they flow freely, quaffed u n t o n a u s e a. He is wont to make banquets vile, breathing out f i l t h,*
1795 *belching w i n e, and pouring out p o i s o n.* This last example is in Sidonius' manner. An adjective is,

— by more than one noun

indeed, accompanied more effectively by two nouns, as is apparent in this example: *The table cover wins approval, lovely i n i t s n e w n e s s a n d w h i t e n e s s; the food prepared w i t h c o s t l i n e s s*
1800 *a n d s k i l l; the drink delicious i n i t s w i n e a s i n n e c t a r; the attendant notable i n m a n n e r a n d a p p a r e l. Graciousness in giving, and the countenance of the giver constitute the double glory of a feast.*

By a similar principle, I join nouns in the nominative case with verbs, thus: *Now my s k i n
shrivels, my h e a r t palpitates, my l u n g s gasp for
breath, my l o i n s stiffen, my b a c k curves, my b o d y
trembles, and death stands at the threshold.* Or I join a
nominative case with a verb in the following way:
*He comprehends l i k e   C a t o, speaks l i k e   C i c e r o,
acts vigorously l i k e   P y r r h u s, shines l i k e   P a r i s,
dares l i k e   C a p a n e u s, loves l i k e   T h e s e u s,
makes music l i k e   O r p h e u s.* Or again, you may
use oblique cases of the noun, thus: *He blazes
w i t h   a n g e r, terrifies w i t h   a   l o o k, thunders
i n   s p e e c h, threatens w i t h   h i s   s w o r d, rages
i n   h i s   g e s t u r e s.* Or multiply clauses in this
way: *Divine goodness, pitying the contrite heart, forgives
trespasses, remits sin, implants love of itself, and promises the joys of true life; but man loses this unless he
perseveres in his love.* Or you may find appropriate
adverbs for verbs, thus: *The actor gorges e a r l y,
drinks a v i d l y, spends r e c k l e s s l y, lives s h a m e-
f u l l y.* Or again, try a variety of determinations
in this way: *He gathers the dice swiftly, examines them
shrewdly, shakes them deftly, throws them vigorously,
cajoles them amicably, waits the outcome composedly.
When they are favourably cast he remains placidly cool,
he smiles at unlucky throws; in neither case is his temper
disturbed, in the one and the other he is philosophic.*
This is the usual style of Sidonius; the extended
series of clauses is an excellent technique. To
extend them thus is appropriate for verse in two
instances: panegyric and denunciation. In panegyric, multiple clauses heighten the praise, and in
denunciation they act as a mallet to strike repeated
blows. The pen of Sidonius claims as its distinctive

Determination of
a verb

— by a noun in
the nominative

1805

1810 — or in an
oblique case

1815

— by an adverb

— by a variety
of determina-
tions

1820

1825

1830

mark this practice of amplifying verse by introducing numerous clauses. The very different
style of Seneca is far removed from the practice
of Sidonius: *He is free who serves not vice; rich, who*
1835 *finds what he has sufficient; poor, who desires more.*
This is Seneca's manner, bringing his line to a
swift conclusion. Both authors, it is true, deserve
honour; but which should I follow, the former or
the latter? Since freshness is a source of greater
pleasure, and sameness of manner wearies us,
I shall not be like the latter, nor yet like the former;
1840 I shall not be exclusively either diffuse or concise;
rather, I shall be both concise and diffuse, becoming
both of these authors by being neither.

5. *Various Prescriptions*

Choice of words

(a) according to
persons and
circumstances

If you heed the directives carefully and suit words
to content, you will speak with precise appropri-
ateness in this way. If mention has perhaps arisen
of an object, sex, age, condition, event, place, or
1845 time, it is regard for its distinctive quality that
the object, sex, age, condition, event, time, or
place claims as its due. Felicity in this matter is an
admirable thing, for when I make an apt use of
qualifying words [*determino*] I give the whole theme
a finished completeness [*termino*]. An object described [*condīta*] in its entirety is a dish well-seasoned
1850 [*condīta*]. Note this prescription and heed its
tenor; it is a prescription that is valid for prose as
well as for verse. The same principle of art holds
good for both, although in a different way.

(b) according to
the requirements
of verse

Metre is straitened by laws, but prose roams
along a freer way, for the public road of prose
1855 admits here and there wagons and carts, whereas

the narrow path of a line of verse does not allow
of things so inelegant. Verse wishes its very words
to be graceful in appearance, lest the rustic form
of a word embarrass by its ungainliness, and bring
shame to the line. Metre desires to appear as a
handmaid with hair adorned, with shining cheek, 1860
slim body, and peerless form. The charming grace-
fulness of verse cannot find a group of words of
equal sweetness to the ear. A line of prose is a
coarser thing; it favours all words, observing no
distinction except in the case of those which it
keeps for the end of periods: such words are those
whose penultimate syllable carries the accent. 1865
It is not desirable that other words hold this final
position. Aulus Gellius reaches the same conclusion
and subjoins his reason: lest otherwise the number
of syllables be weak and insufficient to bring the
line to a close. If the last word of a period should
be, as it frequently is, of a different cursus, never- 1870
theless the one suggested above is preferable
in as much as sounder opinion supports it — and
my authority here is Aulus Gellius. For the rest,
the method of prose and verse does not differ;
rather, the principles of art remain the same, 1875
whether in a composition bound by the laws of
metre or in one independent of those laws, although what depends upon the principles of art
is not always the same. In both prose and verse
see that diction is controlled in such a way that
words do not enter as dry things, but let their meaning
confer a juicy savour upon them, and let them
arrive succulent and rare. Let them say nothing
in a childish way; see that they have dignity but
not pomposity, lest what should be honourable 1880

becomes onerous. Do not let them enter with unsightly mien; rather, see that there is both internal and external adornment. Let the hand of artistic skill provide colours of both kinds.

Comic style   Yet there are times when adornment consists in avoiding ornaments, except such as ordinary speech employs and colloquial use allows. A
1885 comic subject rejects diction that has been artfully laboured over; it demands plain words only. The following comic tale makes this clear in a few lines:

Three of us are sharing expenses and we have no servant. We lay down this rule, that we are to prepare
1890 *our own meals, each man in his turn. After the other two have had their turn to serve, the third day comes round and meal time calls me. I use my breath for bellows to make the fire. The water supply is down and demands replenishing. I grab a jug and look for the spring. There is a stone in my path; my foot slips; the jug is broken.*
1895 *Now two things are lacking — a jug and water. What am I to do? While I'm thinking it over, I go into the market. A man is sitting there with jugs all around him. As I'm turning over in my hands and examining jugs I have picked up he, seeing I am poor, fears a theft and*
1900 *shouts a tme in rough language. I go off, embarrassed, come upon a friend, and tell him my story. "I'll go back to him," I say, "and you follow me and announce the death of my father." I disguise myself and go back to the place. I pick up a jug in one hand, a second jug in the other. My friend calls out and says: "What are you*
1905 *doing? Whatever are you doing here? Poor fellow, your father, who was sick, has died — and are you hanging around here, you dolt?" At that "has died" my grip, as I clasp my hands together, smashes the jugs. I run away.*

I confound the boorish fellow who shamed me, and pay back his insulting words in this way.

A comic discourse is marked with the character 1910 of lightness in the following ways: levity of spirit is the source of comedy; comedy is an immature form, attractive to green years. Moreover, the subject of comedy is light; to such a subject the sportive period of youth readily devotes itself. See to it that the third element is light. Let all aspects, then, be light: the whole is in perfect 1915 harmony if the spirit is light, and the subject light, and the expression light.

If you are treating of serious matters, let the style be serious and the spirit serious, the thought mature and the expression mature. Adorn both thought and expression in the ways prescribed above.

It is, however, of primary importance to clear 1920   Faults to avoid away from the poem what is unsightly, and to root out what is faulty. Recall briefly what things, what kind of things, and how many things render the flow of discourse faulty. *Ecce deae aethereae advenere*:   1 hiatus the hiatus of sound in this sequence of words is appalling. Artistic theory has given as a law to vowels that there be no concentrated sequence of 1925 them. It tolerates a sequence, but forbids a concentrated sequence; and the particular grouping of vowels above, because it is concentrated, is ugly, and constitutes an extreme example of hiatus.

Tu, Tite, tuta te virtute tuente tueris: the graceless   2 excessive and too frequent repetition of a single letter is a   repetition of   a letter cause for censure, whereas tactful repetition is a 1930 grace.

3 excessive repeti-
tion of a word

Cum non sit ratio rationis de ratione, hinc non est ratio praebere fidem rationi: a word is cheapened when it is repeated so frequently and inanely. The moderate repetition of words is an adornment; whatever is

1935 excessive is a thing remote from adornment.

4 excessive repeti-
tion of word-
endings

Repetition of the same word-endings is sometimes a grace; an excessive number of such sounds is graceless: *infantes, stantes, lacrimantes, vociferantes.* These four defects result in a faulty style. There is

5 excessively long
periods

1940

a fifth defect when too long a period is held in suspension. A sixth is added to these when the

6 incongruous word
order

transposed order of a word appears incongruous, as here: *Luci misimus Aeli.*

Now, I have provided a comb: if they are groomed with it, compositions, whether in prose or verse, will gleam with elegance. But whether or not you make good use of the comb, you will be able to

1945 discern beauty of form clearly in this mirror.

The triple judge-
ment of mind, ear,
and good usage

When you examine the appearance of a word to see whether some lurking blemish may mar it, do not let the ear be the sole judge, nor the mind be sole judge; let a triple judgement of mind and ear and usage decide the matter. This is my method

1950 when I am labouring to polish words: I chide my mind, lest it linger in one place, for the quiet of standing water makes it stagnant. Rather, with unflagging energy I turn now in one direction, now in another, and I adorn the subject now with one figure, now with another. I do not turn it over in my mind once only; rather, I reconsider it many

1955 times. At last the active mind, when it has completed its circuit, chooses one form out of many. It breathes freely at what it considers a flawless position. But in many cases the augur is mistaken;

as long as words lie buried deep in the understanding, many seem good to the mind which the ear,
on its part, fails to approve.

See to it that an expression, as it wins the mind's 1960
approval, may likewise charm the ear, and the two
approve the same thing. Even that is not sufficient, and I still do not trust it unless I reflect upon
it again. A first examination discerns neither well
nor fully. As I revolve the subject, I evolve more.
If the topic is malodorous, its unpleasantness is
intensified as it is moved about more; if it is full 1965
of savour, the taste is more delightful through repeated testing. See, then, that there are three
judges of the proposed expression: let the mind be
the first judge, the ear the second, and usage the
third and final one to conclude the whole.

V. Memory

If you wish to remember all that reason invents,
or order disposes, or adornment refines, keep in 1970
mind this counsel, valuable though brief: the little
cell that remembers is a cell of delights, and it
craves what is delightful, not what is boring. Do
you wish to gratify it ? Do not burden it. It desires
to be treated kindly, not hard pressed. Because 1975
memory is a slippery thing, and is not capable of
dealing with a throng of objects, feed it in the
following way. When you appease hunger, do not
be so sated with food that you can have nothing
further set before you. Be more than half, but less
than fully satisfied. Give to your stomach not as
much as it can hold, but as much as is beneficial; 1980
nature is to be nourished, not overburdened. To

remain between satiety and hunger is the wiser
practice. So, too, in drinking, you moderate drink
in accordance with reason. Sip, do not swill; let
drink be taken in an honourable [*honori*], not an
1985 onerous [*oneri*] fashion. Drink as a temperate man,
not a tippler. The abstemious man arraigns wine
with better grace than the drunkard refutes him.
Knowledge, which is the food and drink of the
mind, should be tasted in accordance with the
same rule. Let it feed the mind in such a way
that it is offered as a delight, not a burden to it.
1990 Suppose you are to learn this entire discourse:
divide it into very small parts. Do not take several
at once; rather, take one at a time, a very short
section, much shorter than your shoulders are
capable and desirous of bearing. In this way
there will be pleasure, and nothing burdensome in
the burden. Let practice come as companion;
1995 while the matter is fresh and new go over it frequently and repeat it; then stop, rest for a little
while, take a breathing space. After a short delay
has intervened, another piece may be summoned
up; when it has been memorized in the same way,
let practice join both parts together in the cell
2000 mentioned above, let it consolidate them and
cement them together. Join a third part to these
two with a similar bond, and a fourth part to the
other three. But, in following through these steps,
you make a mistake if you do not consistently
proceed in such a way that you stop short of weari-
ness. This advice holds good for all the faculties
2005 of sense; it sharpens those that are dull, makes
pliable those that ,are rigid, and raises to greater
heights of excellence those that are acute and

flexible. Whatever attempts more than these precepts accomplishes less. Therefore let this sound principle adapt to each man the weight he can bear, and be the one model for all.

To these methods add others which I make use of — and which it is expedient to use. When I wish to recall things I have seen, or heard, or 2010 memorized before, or engaged in before, I ponder thus: I saw, I heard, I considered, I acted in such or such a way, either at that time or in that place: places, times, images, or other similar signposts are for me a sure path which leads me to the things 2015 themselves. Through these signs I arrive at active knowledge. Such and such a thing was so, and I picture to myself such and such a thing.

Cicero relies on unusual images as a technique for training the memory; but he is teaching himself; and let the subtle teacher, as it were in solitude, address his subtlety to himself alone. But my own subtlety may be pleasing to me and not to him. 2020 It is beneficial to one whom it suits, for enjoyment alone makes the power of memory strong. Therefore have no faith in these or in other signposts if they are difficult for you, or if they are unacceptable. But if you wish to proceed with greater security, fashion signs for yourself, whatever kind your own 2025 inclination suggests. As long as they give you pleasure, you may be taught through their means. There are some men who wish to know, but not to make an effort, nor to endure the concentration and pain of learning. That is the way of the cat; it wants the fish, but not the fishing. I am not addressing myself to such men, but to those who delight in knowing, and also in the effort of 2030 acquiring knowledge.

VI. DELIVERY

In reciting aloud, let three tongues speak:
let the first be that of the mouth, the second that
of the speaker's countenance, and the third that of
gesture. The voice has its own laws, and you should
observe them in this way: the period that is spoken
should observe its natural pauses, and the word its
2035 accent. Separate those words which the sense
separates, join those that sense joins. Modulate your
voice in such a way that it is in harmony with the
subject; and take care that voice does not advance
along a path different from that which the subject
follows. Let the two go together; let the voice be,
as it were, a reflection of the subject. As the nature
2040 of your subject is, so let your voice be when you
rehearse it: let us recognize them as one.

Anger, child of fire and mother of fury, springing
up from the very bellows, poisons the heart and
soul. It stings with its bellows, sears with its fire,
convulses with its fury. Under its emotion, a caustic
2045 voice speaks; an inflamed countenance and tur-
bulent gestures accompany it. The outward emotion corresponds with the inward; outer and inner
man are affected alike. If you act the part of this
man, what, as reciter, will you do ? Imitate genuine fury, but do not be furious. Be affected
2050 in part as he is, but not deeply so. Let your manner
be the same in every respect, but not so extreme;
yet suggest, as is fitting, the emotion itself. You can
represent the manner of a rustic and still be graceful: let your voice represent his voice; your facial
expression, his own; and your gesture his gesture —
by recognizable signs. This is a carefully tempered

skill; this method is attractive in the tongue that 2055
recites, and this food is a delight to the ear. Therefore, let a voice controlled by good taste, seasoned
with the two spices of facial expression and gesture,
be borne to the ears to feed the hearing. Strength
issues from the tongue, for death and life depend
upon the powers of the tongue, if haply it is aided 2060
by the tempering principles of facial expression
and gesture. So, then, let all be in harmony:
suitable invention, flowing expression, polished
development, firm retention in memory. If dis-
courses are delivered ineptly, they are no more to be
praised than is a recitation charmingly delivered 2065
but without the other requirements mentioned.

Epilogue

Now I have crossed the sea; I have fixed my
Cadiz on the shore. And I resolve upon you as my
goal, you who, greatest of creatures, are neither
God nor yet man. You are neither — yet some-
where between the two: one whom God has chosen
as his partner. He deals with you as an associate,
sharing the world with you. It was not his will to 2070
possess all things — he alone; rather, he willed
earth to be yours and heaven his own. What
better thing could he do, what greater ? For what
better or what greater man ? I put it more moderately, for what man as great, or what man like
to you ? Therefore, Father, vicar of Christ, I
commend myself wholly to you, you whose wisdom 2075
is like a full-flowing fountain, whose keenness of
mind is like a fire throwing out sparks, whose ready
eloquence is a swift-flowing torrent, and whose

grace is a marvel. Transcending all that is human,
2080 I would wish to speak freely, but the reality is far
richer than speech.

Crown of the empire, you whom Rome, capitol
of the world, serves with bent knee; you who, rich
in the sweet nectar of the muses, give forth fragrance
tempered with the perfume of your manners,
with your leave I shall speak, and briefly. Although
you are able to do most things, be pleased to retain
2085 only the power to do them. Take care to imprint
on your mind: although you can inflict injury,
do not wish to; the power to injure is already
injury enough. Do nothing which you would
afterwards wish undone, but let deliberation be the
cautious prelude to action. Do you not see, if you
regard the true qualities of our prince, that he
2090 has become the soldier of the cross and of Christ,
and sword of the entire church? Devotion so great
calls for love, not for hatred; for praise, not reproach; for rewards and not penalties. Therefore,
you who conquer all else, allow yourself to be
conquered here. Be pleased to turn, and desire the
2095 king to return. Flower and crown of the clergy,
with wonted sweetness the richest honeycombs
drop their dew from your heart [grant me a share
of your honey's sweetness]. I plead for our prince.
I am least of men, you are greatest; yet be receptive,
and let him fare better in his role of suppliant.

Second dedication   Accept, O flower of the kingdom, this special
gift of a little book which I have written for the
2100 pope. Receive the highest honour this private
work offers. And take not the book alone, William,
man of gold, but with it I give you all that I am;
I am wholly yours as a votive offering. Your heart,

generous in all things, is not ensnared by trifles, but ever aspires on high. Nobility in giving, which 2105 men of this age do not know, is inborn in you, jewel of donors, who alone so give that in giving no hand is more lavish, no mind happier, no hesitation so brief. You are the man upon whom alone God has bestowed every gift that is fitting, as on one with a mind of great wisdom — one on whose 2110 mind the minds of kings are wont to rely in carrying on the affairs of the kingdom. You are great in giving, prudent in doing, modest in bearing, inflexible in law, in everything faithful; and divine power, going before you, ever fosters your success, and you ever rise towards the heights. But if every peak of honour should rise higher for you, 2115 you could not rise in honour as much as you justly deserve.

TEXTUAL NOTES

After a preliminary examination of twenty-three manuscripts of the *Poetria Nova*, I made careful and extensive use of the following while preparing this translation:

Corpus Christi College, Cambridge, 406; 13thC.
Trinity College, Cambridge, 609 (R.3.29); early 13thC.
Trinity College, Cambridge, 624 (R.3.51); early 13thC.
Trinity College, Cambridge, 895 (R.14.22); 13thC.
Bodleian Library, Laud Miscellany 515; early 13thC.
British Museum, Harley 3582; 13thC.
Harley 6504; 15thC.
Add. MS 18153; 14thC.
Add. MS 21214; 14thC.
Add. MS 37495; 14thC.

In the list that follows, the first form is Faral's reading; the second, the reading I adopted, with strong manuscript support. I have not indicated variant readings unless they affect translation (e.g. at 1.20 *hominem* is almost universal in the MSS, where Faral reads *homines*); nor do I list changes in punctuation from Faral's edition, even though this does, at times, affect the meaning.

65	illud: illam
261	sic: sed
285	vicisse: fecisse
300	cunctis: aliis
	crede: finge
305	opere: ope
329	fides: sedes
	regmine: remige
369	planctu: gestu
427	facta: facti
452	punge: pinse
483	foret: fuit
486	respice: resipisce
517	gravis: Gallis

525	doloris: timoris
645	hinc: huic
652	fragilem: facilem
706	inducet: inducat
748	admotă: admotō
872	vincet: vincit
1025	comperit: reperit
1034	augustus: angustus
1112	Suasit mihi rem non esse nocivam. — Quare...: Suasit. Rem noscens esse nocivam, quare...
1139	auctor: hostis
1184	emisit: amisit
1188	purum vinceret hostis: purus promptius esset
1205	quod: qui
1230	autem: alii
1239	possent: possunt
1274	demonstro: si monstro
1318	dono: pleno
1384	si tandem forte venimus: vel si fortasse venimus
1388	ungue (emended by Faral in his *errata*, p. 384, to angue): *stet* ungue
1395	rebellis: rebelli
1400	salvabit: salvavit
1407	spreta: sputa
1410	redemit: peremit
1458	die: dies
1537	se... re: re... se
1541	minima: nimia
1576	voluit: noluit
1586	surget: surgit
1597	quasi: ne quasi
1621	discernat: discernas
1626	doloris: dolori
1644	sententia: transumptio
1657	coruscat: coruscant
1664	sumas: sumes
1675	vocisque: vocesque
1680	sit: stet
1695	nudam: crudam
1786	rerumque: retinensque
1791	mensas: epulas
1902	proclama: proclames

1930	minus: nimis
1942	lusimus Elyn: misimus Eli
1968	qui terminet: qui totum terminet
1976	ad... turbas: et turbae
1983	potas: potans
2079	transcendes: transcendens
2112	Cf. Faral's textual notes. I have read:

Magnus es in dando, prudens in agendo, modestus
In gestu, rigidus in iure, fidelis in omni
Re, semperque tuos divina praeambula virtus
Urget successus...

EXPLANATORY NOTES

Dedication: The adulation of this prologue, addressed to Pope Innocent III, remains well within the conventions of medieval panegyric. The topic of "outdoing," and the related *taceat* and *cedat* formulas ("Let Lucan now be mute, mute Ovid too!" *Inferno* xxv, 94), were extremely common in the Middle Ages and much later. So, too, was the "aged youth" topic (a favourite of Geoffrey's; cf. 20-27, 174-79, 674-86, 1309-10). Innocent III had been elected pope at the age of thirty-seven.

1-8   *Innŏcēns* presents an impossible combination of syllables for the dactyllic hexameter line. Similar playing on metrically difficult proper names was common in medieval Latin poetry. More significant is the fact that a number of technical rhetorical terms present similar metrical difficulty, and Geoffrey has been forced to seek periphrases which are sometimes far from clear.

31   *England sent me to Rome*: Professor C. R. Cheney of Corpus Christi College, Cambridge, has assured me that Geoffrey of Vinsauf's name does not occur in any of the documents relating to the complicated dealings of England with the Papal court during the reign of John. If Geoffrey was a member of any official mission to Rome, it was in a very minor capacity.

43-70   Geoffrey of Vinsauf introduces at the beginning of his treatise the basic rhetorical distinction between *res* and *verba*: the poem as intellectual construct and the poem as verbal construct. He devotes little formal attention to the first of these, assuming that here the poet's craft does not differ from the prose writer's. In his "model exercises," however, he covers a range of possible material for the poet, from scriptural story and commentary through *contemptus mundi* themes, devotional verse, elegy, eulogy, complaint, description, anecdote, to satire and comedy.

43-45   Cf. Chaucer's *Troilus and Criseyde*, I, 1065-69.

47   *The mind's hand*: Geoffrey makes frequent use of corporal metaphors (e.g. 46, 55, 111, 721, 778, 1062, 1225, 1615). At times the effect is grotesque to modern ears ("the hand of the

tongue," 1.2060), but the corporal metaphor had a respected history throughout the classical and medieval periods.

56   *order*: For metrical reasons, Geoffrey consistently uses the term *ordo* for the more technical rhetorical term *dispositio*.

57   *Gades*: limit. Vid. Juvenal, x, 1.

63-65   *head, body, final details*: Geoffrey refers, again in a corporal metaphor, to the three parts of a composition: beginning, middle, end.

80   *the path:* i.e. natural order or the order of art.

81   *with what scales:* i.e. amplified or abbreviated treatment, as the dignity of the subject demands.

127   *proverb*: Geoffrey understands by the term *proverbium* (synonyms: *sententia*, 1.127; *hoc generale*, 1.180: *istud commune*, 1.185) any general truth drawn from observation or experience.

143   *exempla*: The term *exemplaris imago* (illustrative image, 1. 193) renders more precise what Geoffrey understands by the term *exemplum*. All the exempla he offers as models in this treatise (ll. 193-202) and in his *Documentum de Modo et Arte Dictandi et Versificandi*, I, 14-17, are exemplary images rather than stories.

146-49   Matthew of Vendôme, e.g., had suggested beginning a poem with zeugma, hypozeuxis, or metonymy (*Ars Versificatoria*, I, 3-15); John of Garland, a younger contemporary of Geoffrey's, suggested a technique of the ancients: invocation and argument (*De arte prosayca et metrica... in Romanische Forschungen*, XIII, 1902, p. 906).

155ff.   *Minos, Androgeos, Scylla*: The story may have had special status in the schools as a type of poetic invention. Cf. Bernard Sylvestris' commentary on the *Aeneid* (VI, 20): "*In foribus: in introitu ad artes: in auctoribus. Letum Androgei: Hae fabulae quae sunt in foribus extra templum figurant omnes poetarum fabulas et ideo non sunt mistice intelligenda.*" ("*On the gates:* at the entrance to the arts: in the authors. *The death of Androgeos:* the fables which are on the gates outside the temple represent all the fables of the poets, and are not to be interpreted mystically.") *Commentum Bernardi Silvestris super sex libros Eneidos Virgilii*, ed. Guilielmus Riedel, Greifswald, 1924, p. 37.

168   The topos of the traitor betrayed, the stinger stung, the poisoner

poisoned, the archer pierced by his own arrow is extremely common in medieval and Renaissance literature. The student unacquainted with classical and medieval rhetoric should acquire some basic knowledge of the very important tradition of the topics as a rich storehouse of poetic invention throughout the Middle Ages and the Renaissance. See, by way of introduction, E. R. Curtius, *European Literature and the Latin Middle Ages*, New York, 1953, especially Chapter Five.

202 A number of manuscripts (e.g. British Museum Royal 12 E xi; Bodleian Selden Supra 65; Durham CIV; et al.) insert at this point a passage of some forty-four lines on ways of passing from the beginning to the body of a work. The passage corresponds closely to the material in the *Documentum de Modo et Arte Dictandi et Versificandi* II, I, 1-12.

220-63 In his treatment of *interpretatio*, *circuitio*, and *collatio*, Geoffrey is at once defining and exemplifying the three processes. Lack of clarity (e.g. after 1.255) results in part from a series of *collationes occultae*, hidden comparisons.

285 *the serpent*: Virgil, *Eclogues*, III, 93.

296 *lay lighter burdens*: cf. Horace, *Ars Poetica*, 40. Geoffrey uses the metaphor again in lines 1086, 1993.

368ff. The lament on the death of Richard is referred to with mocking admiration by Chaucer in the *Nun's Priest's Tale*, 3347 — one of the most richly "rhetorical" of all Chaucer's writings. In fairness to Geoffrey, it should be remembered that the *Ad Herennium* recommended a certain exaggeration in model exercises in order to make the point clearer for students.

377-78 Richard was wounded on Friday, March 26, 1199, and died on April 6, the twelfth day after.

437 *Boys are raised up*: a topos in the twelfth and thirteenth centuries. Cf. the popular lyric in the *Carmina Burana*:

> *At nunc decennes pueri*
> *Decusso iugo liberi*
> *Se nunc magistros jacitant.*

See, also E. Duméril, *Poésies populaires du moyen âge*, Paris, 1847, p. 153; and, in more serious vein, L. J. Paetow, *Battle of the Seven Arts*, Berkeley, 1914, p. 22.

452   *ciconia:* a gesture of derision made by imitating the shape of a stork's bill by bending the fingers.

469   A large number of manuscripts add, after "I, the ravished cross, make my complaint," the following lines: "I, the cross, the cross of Christ crucified, the holy cross, the salvation of men and redemption of the world, I the ravished cross, make my complaint."

475   Here, too, after "...without an avenger," many manuscripts add: "you, for whose welfare I bore that load, whom I thus redeemed from death ? Could I thus become vile in your eyes ?"

515-26   This passage is probably a reference to Château-Gaillard, built at the order of King Richard to defend Normandy against Philip II of France. Completed in 1198, it seemed, by reason of its site, all but impregnable; however, it was taken after a six-month siege in 1204. Apparently, then, this passage of the *Poetria Nova* was written between 1198 and the end of 1203. The entire passage is missing from many manuscripts, however, and its significance for the dating of this work as a whole remains unclear.

520   There is a slip in the line-numbering of M. Faral's edition here ; it has been allowed to stand in order to facilitate reference.

545-48   The topos of *Mater Terra- Pater Aether* appears frequently in classical and medieval times.

625   *the image of milk:* In the context of Geoffrey's habits of expression, the two most likely meanings for this odd figure are: (1) white bread, an interpretation perhaps supported by the clause that follows: "Ceres is honoured" (and cf. ll. 765-76, and Juvenal, v. 70); and (2) white tablecloth (cf. ll. 1768-72). Two manuscripts gloss *lactis imago* as *mappa* or *mensale,* i.e. table covering, one manuscript glosses it *panis albus.*

645   *castanets:* Du Cange records only this use of the word *tabella* as a musical instrument. The context, and the phrase *gemina ludente tabella,* suggest something in the nature of castanets or, as Mr. W. B. Sedgwick suggests, tambourines. Cf. Italian *tabella.*

713ff.   The story of the snow child was a popular theme in the Middle Ages. In addition to M. Faral's reference, see E. Duméril, *Poésies inédites du moyen âge,* p. 418; and M. Manitius, *Geschichte der lateinischen Literatur des Mittelalters,* III, 1035.

747   *It is a picture:* Horace, *Ars Poetica*, 360ff.

758ff.   The word's "native soil" (*proprium locum*) refers to its literal meaning rather than to its position in the sentence. To "take up an abode on the estate of another" is to assume metaphorical meaning. Cf. Quintilian VIII, vi, 5 on metaphor: "A noun or a verb is transferred from the place to which it properly belongs to another where there is either no literal term or the transferred term is better than the literal."

766-67   This statement, difficult and condensed in the Latin, is expanded at some length in the *Documentum* II, 3, 15-18. I have read *expresse* for *expressae*.

844-52   Geoffrey's habit of combining example with precept is well illustrated here. His instructions on the use of the verb as metaphor incorporate the following "transposed" verbs: *sedeat, veniat, succurrat, serenet, illuminet, transfundat, lucet, latet.*

949-1060 In his discussion of the "difficult figures of diction," or tropes, Geoffrey follows closely the treatment, although not the order, of the *Ad Herennium*, IV, xxxi, 42-xxxiv, 46. He states that there are ten such figures but omits mention of the tenth, *circumitio* or periphrasis.

1098ff.   For each of the thirty-five "figures of words" exemplified by Geoffrey under the heading "easy ornament" I append a brief definition, along with the Greek equivalent if it has entered into English usage. The definitions are based on Geoffrey's source, the *Ad Herennium*, IV, xii, 18-xxx, 41.

1098   *repetitio* [epanaphora]: repetition of a word at the beginning of successive clauses.

1099   *conversio* [antistrophe]: repetition of a word at the end of successive clauses.

1100   *complexio*: repetition of both initial and final words in successive clauses.

1101   *traductio*: (a) use of words with the same sound, but different meaning or function; or (b) repetition of a single word, preferably in different cases.

1103   *contentio* [antithesis]: a statement built on contraries.

1105   *exclamatio* [apostrophe]: an expression of grief or indignation, addressed to a person, place, or object.

1107   *interrogatio*: summing up the case against an adversary, together with a challenging question.

1110   *ratiocinatio*: reasoning by question and answer.

1117   *sententia*: a maxim or general observation, showing what does or should happen in life.

1118   *contrarium*: reasoning by contraries; implying the answer to a question by appealing to another position not open to question.

1120   *membrum* [colon]: two, or preferably three, succinct clauses, each complete in itself, but joined to express a total meaning.

1122   *articulus* [comma]: a series of single words without connectives, giving a staccato effect.

1124   *continuatio* [period]: a compact group of words expressing with great directness a complete thought (a) *in sententia*: in a maxim; (b) *in contrario*: in a contrast; (c) *in occlusione*: in a conclusion.

1128   *compar* [isocolon]: clauses with a virtually equal number of syllables. (The example given omits from the count *ne forte* "lest perchance").

1130   *similiter cadens*: [homoeoptoton]: two or more words with the same case endings, within one sentence.

1132   *similiter desinens* [homoeoteleuton]: two or more indeclinable words with the same endings, within one sentence.

1135   *adnominatio* [paronomasia]: word-play depending upon a slight change or transposition of letters, or the addition of a prefix, or a variation in word form or case.

1139   *subjectio* [hypophora]: a question or series of questions put to an adversary, with answers subjoined that destroy his case.

1145   *gradatio* [climax]: repetition of the closing word of one clause as the opening word of the next. A second form of climax is mentioned in *Ad Herennium*, IV, xxv, 34, and exemplified: "...if they may do what they please, and can do what they may, and dare do what they can..."

1153   *definitio*: a brief and pointed summary of the characteristic quality of a person or thing.

1155   *transitio*: a brief recalling of what has been said, and an introduction to what is to follow.

1157   *correctio* [epanorthosis]: retraction of what has just been said, and substitution of a more suitable word.

1159   *occupatio* [paralipsis]: description of a situation, or naming of objects, while professing to leave them unmentioned through lack of knowledge, or unwillingness to discuss them; also called *occultatio*.

1163   *disjunctio* (or *disjunctum*): position of verbs at the end of each of two or more clauses.

1166   *conjunctio*: position of a single verb between two clauses, linking those clauses.

1167   *adjunctio*: position of a verb (a) at the beginning of the first of two clauses, controlling both clauses; or (b) at the end of the second of two clauses, controlling both clauses.

1169   *conduplicatio*: repetition of one or more words for amplification or pity.

1173   *interpretatio* [synonymy]: repetition of a single idea in synonymous words.

1174   *commutatio*: parallel phrasing, with transposed order of words in the two halves of the statement. The *Ad Herennium* states that the two parts of the statement are antithetical; this is not so in Geoffrey's example.

1175   *permissio*: surrender of the total situation to the will of another.

1179   *dubitatio*: expression of uncertainty as to which of two or more words is most suitable.

1186   *expeditio*: enumeration of various alternatives, and rejection of all but one.

1201   *dissolutio* or *dissolutum* [asyndeton]: a concise series of clauses without connectives.

1213   *praecisio* [aposiopesis]: the breaking off of a sentence, for emotional effect or implication.

1215   *conclusio*: a brief argument deducing the necessary consequences of what has been said or done.

1249-50   The three ways of "saying the same thing with variations," according to the *Ad Herennium*, IV, xlii, 54, are: (1) with merely verbal changes; (2) with changes in the tone of delivery; (3) with changes of treatment; i.e. with dialogue (*sermocinatio, P.N.* 1305ff), or with arousal (*exsuscitatio,* P.N.1325ff).

The seven ways of elaborating upon a theme (*Ad Herennium,* IV, xliii, 56-57) are exemplified by Geoffrey at lines 1327-44. The reference to Cicero, l. 1251, is, of course, to the *Ad Herennium,* which was accepted as Cicero's all through the Middle Ages.

1345   At this point Geoffrey gives no example of *commoratio;* he is following the precedent set by the *Ad Herennium,* IV, xlv, 58, which states that *commoratio* is not separable from the composition as a whole, but flows through it as blood flows through the body.

1407-10 These four lines, missing in a number of manuscripts, are possibly spurious.

1583   Five species of *significatio* are mentioned here, although marginal annotations list six types. The discrepancy in number is probably due to the fact that only five are noted in the *Ad Herennium;* Geoffrey's first type, *diminutio,* is not listed there as a variety of *significatio,* but only as a separate figure of thought. (*Ad Herennium,* IV, xxxviii, 50. Cf. P.N., 1236 and 1285).

1588-1841 The two sections on conversions (ll. 1588-1760) and determinations (ll. 1761-1841) have no equivalent in Geoffrey's major source, the *Ad Herennium,* but represent a complex relationship of disciplines of major importance in the twelfth and thirteenth centuries. Artificial and pedestrian as these sections seems today, they recall the vital connections (approaching at times identity) between rhetoric, poetics and grammar. The subject is far too vast to outline in a note; one of the most illuminating texts to turn to for an initial insight into this complicated matter is John of Salisbury's famous account of the teaching methods of Bernard of Chartres: "Bernard of Chartres, the richest fount of literary learning in modern times, taught the authors in this way: he pointed out what was simple, and what conformed to rule; he called attention to grammatical figures, rhetorical colours, and sophistic fallacies; he showed where a given text was related to other disciplines. Yet in teaching he did not labour the text; rather, he gave by stages to his listeners what was commensurate with

their capacities. He took every opportunity to impress upon
his hearers the fact that excellence of expression depends upon
the quality of *proprietas* (the precise adaptation of adjective and
verb to noun), or on metaphor (the transferring of a word from
one sense to another, by reason of acceptable affinities between
them). Since practice strengthens the memory and sharpens
the mind, he urged all (some by encouragement, some by
penalties) to imitate what they heard. He required each of
them to report the next day something he had heard the
previous day.... The evening exercise, the *declinatio*, was so
strong on drilling grammar that anyone who worked throughout
the year (unless he was stupid) had a grasp of the art of speaking
and writing, and could not be ignorant of the meaning of expressions in current use.... He expounded the poets and orators
to those of his students who were assigned as preliminary exercises the imitation of works in prose or verse. Pointing out
skilful connections between words and elegant closing rhythms,
he would urge his students to follow in the steps of the authors....
He bade them reproduce the very image of the authors, and
succeeded in making a student who imitated the great writers
himself worthy of posterity's imitation. He also taught, among
his first lessons, the merits of economy, and the laudable adornment of thought and expression. He pointed out what constitutes meagre thinness of style, or acceptable richness, or extravagance; and moderation in all matters. He urged his students to read stories and poems, attentively and without hurry,
and required of each that he commit something to memory
each day." (*Metalogicon*, ed. Clemens Webb, Oxford, 1929;
I, xxiv, pp. 55-56).

Teaching methods similar to Bernard's were in use at Orleans and at Paris where Geoffrey studied. Edmond Faral
suggests that the explication of such a poet as Sidonius Apolli-
naris might well contribute to the grammatical acrobatics of
this part of the *Poetria Nova*.

1740-42 The allusion here has not been certainly identified. There
may be echoes from Aristotle's *Problemata* 5.25 (Bekker, 881b,
l. 3) transmitted to Geoffrey indirectly. Mr. W. B. Sedgwick
calls attention to the proverb: *Pluribus intentus minor est ad singula
sensus*. The lines that follow are far from clear; the point of
Geoffrey's example at l. 1745ff. seems to be the reduction of
uninflected words to a minimum.

1796   Similar passages of vituperation or praise in an ornate amplified style are extremely common in Sidonius. Vid.e.g. *Epistles*, II, 1.

1807-09   *Cato... Orpheus*: instances of the "exemplary figures" (*eikon, imago*) recommended by Cicero (*De oratore* I, 18), and Quintilian (XII, 4), and employed very widely in medieval poetry, both Latin and vernacular. Cf. ll. 632-33, 932-35, 1775-6.

1820-25   The lines are a close imitation of Sidonius' description of the Gothic King, Theodoric (*Epistles* I, ii, 7ff): "*...tesseras colligit rapide, inspicit sollicite, volvit argute, mittit instanter, ioculanter compellat, patienter expectat. In bonis jactibus tacet, in malis ridet, in neutris irascitur, in utrisque philosophatur.*"

1843   The words *proprie* in this line, and *proprietas* in l. 1846 carry a weight of meaning. Geoffrey expands upon this important quality of style in the *Documentum* II, 3, 132-139, where it is apparent that his source is Horace's *Ars Poetica*. *Proprietas* is a form of decorum, but recognizes a certain uniqueness in the nature and circumstances of each object the poet approaches, demanding a selection of specifically relevant details, and appropriate diction. Since *proprietas* covers every significant aspect of character: age, education, occupation, natural disposition, tone of voice, quality of diction — the exploiting of its potentialities might well have provided an important training for dramatists in the Renaissance.

1867   Mr. W. B. Sedgwick, in *Speculum*, II, 336-340 identified the reference to Aulus Gellius I, 7, 20: "*Verba sunt haec ipsius ex oratione, quam De imperio Cn Pompei habuit : ' Testis est Silicia quam, multis undique cinctam periculis, non terrore belli sed consilii celeritate explicavit.' At si 'explicuit' diceret, imperfecto et debili numero verborum sonus clauderet.*" Cf. Aulus Gellius, IV, 7, 1-5, on Valerius Probus' pronunciation of *Hannibalem, Hasdrubalem, Hamilcarem* on the second last syllable to improve the rhythm.

1888ff.   For the story, *De tribus sociis*, which, in its verse form, is probably original with Geoffrey, see Manitius III, pp. 1034-35; and R. Jahnke, *Comoediae Horatianae Tres*, Leipzig, 1891, pp. 105-6.

1923   "Lo, the heavenly goddesses have come."

1928   The line obviously dazzled scribal eyes. Manuscript readings vary from the Corpus Christi College's: "*Tite Tati tute tibi tanta tiranne tulisti;*" (a very close imitation of the line from

Ennius' *Annals*, I, quoted in the *Ad Herennium* IV, xii, 18: "*O Tite, tute, Tati, tibi tanta, tyranne, tulisti;*") to innumerable variations on the line as Faral's edition gives it.

1931 "Since the reasonableness of the reason is not clear to reason, it is not reasonable to trust the reason."

1942 The correct reading is surely a phrase from the *Punic War* of L. Caelius Antipater, quoted in the *Ad Herennium* IV, xii, 18: "*In priore libro has res ad te scriptas Luci misimus Aeli.*" ("In the previous book, Lucius Aelius, we sent you an account of these events").

1969ff. On memory as a major part of rhetoric, cf. *Ad Herennium* III, xvi, 29-xxiv, 40; *De Oratore* 2, 85, 350-88; Quintilian II, 2, 1-51.

1986 The source of this rather obscure line is Sidonius' *Epistles* I, ii, 6: "*Scyphorum paterarumque raras oblationes facilius est ut accuset sitis quam recuset ebrietas.*" ("There is more reason for the thirsty to criticize the infrequent filling of goblets than for the intoxicated to refrain from them.")

2017ff. The reference is probably to the *Ad Herennium* III, xx, 33-xxiii, 39. Cf. *De Oratore* II, lxxxvi, 351-lxxxviii, 360.

2031ff. For the extremely important role assigned by rhetoricians to delivery, see *Ad Herennium* III, xi, 19-xv, 27; *Orator* 17, 56; Quintilian XI, 3, (especially XI, 3, 3-6).

2042, 2043. A number of English manuscripts (e.g. Corpus Christi 406, Trinity College Cambridge, 609, 624, 895) read *felle* for *folle* in these two lines — a reading that is very possibly correct (cf. l. 2044: *fellea*).

2081-98 *Crown of the Empire*: This appeal to Pope Innocent III on behalf of King John may refer (as Edmond Faral believed) to John's negotiations for reconciliation with the papacy — negotiations forced less by the interdict on England (1205-12), or by John's excommunication (November, 1209), than by Innocent's move in absolving John's vassals of their allegiance (1212) and inviting Philip of France to lead an army to dethrone him. If this is the period at issue, the date is 1212 — May, 1213. However, as Dr. R. W. Hunt has suggested to me, l.2090 seems to refer to John's taking the cross and enrolling himself in the ranks of the Crusaders (1215) as a means of strengthening his position against the barons. If this is true, the plea may be for Innocent's support of king against barons in the struggle over Magna Carta. In either case, the lines are not definitive in dating the *Poetria Nova;* the entire passage is missing from a great many manuscripts.

2100   *Flower of the kingdom...*, *William.* There have been a number of suggestions, several with the support of manuscript glosses, for the identity of this William. The two strongest probabilities seem to me to be:

(1) William of Wrotham, archdeacon of Taunton, administrator of the navy and the stannaries, a man of great power in England between 1204 and 1215. Dr. R. W. Hunt, Keeper of Western Manuscripts at the Bodleian Library, called my attention to the very important Corpus Christi College Cambridge manuscript (no. 406) of the *Poetria Nova*, dating from the early or mid-thirteenth century, which bears a heading: *Incipit liber magistri Galfridi* [edge of page worn away] *Anglici ad Wlm de Wrotham epistula prima.* On William of Wrotham, see: F. W. Brooks, "William of Wrotham and the Office of Keeper of the King's Ports and Galleys," *English Historical Review* XL (1925), 570-79; and W. R. Powell, "The Administration of the Navy and the Stanneries," *English Historical Review* LXXI (1956), 1189-1216.

(2) William de Sancta Matre Ecclesia, Bishop of London 1199-1221, a trusted adviser of three kings, Henry II, Richard I, and John; and an envoy between the English and Papal courts during the troubled years of John's reign. An excellent Trinity College Cambridge manuscript (no. 895) dating from the first half of the thirteenth century has a gloss at this line (in a mid-thirteenth century hand): *Hic dirigit auctor sermonem ad Willmum episcopum Londonionsem* [sic] *ut eius favore adepta hoc opus in maiori teneatur auctoritate.*